APR 23 1993

COPING WITH

Rejection

COPING WITH

Rejection

JULIA HISLOP

THE ROSEN PUBLISHING GROUP, INC./NEW YORK

Published in 1991 by The Rosen Publishing Group, Inc.
29 East 21st Street, New York, NY 10010

First Edition

Library of Congress Cataloging-in-Publication Data

Hislop, Julia.
    Coping with rejection/Julia Hislop.—1st ed.
      p.   cm.—(Coping)
    Includes bibliographical references and index.
    Summary: Offers practical methods for adolescents in dealing with the emotional issues that surround rejection.
    ISBN 0-8239-1183-7:
    1. Rejection (Psychology)—Juvenile literature. [1. Rejection (Psychology)   2. Emotions.   3. Interpersonal relations.]   I. Title.
II. Series.
BF575.R35H57   1991
158'.2—dc20   90-29123
                                          CIP
                                          AC

Manufactured in the United States of America

*Fondly dedicated
to the
memory of
Rose Baker*

ABOUT THE AUTHOR ◇

J ulia Hislop was raised in Port Huron, Michigan, and attended the University of Michigan, where she studied psychology and received a BA degree in 1984. While completing her undergraduate training, she worked and volunteered in several mental health settings, working with mentally retarded, delinquent, and emotionally disturbed youths and young adults.

Following a year's advanced training in psychology at the Devereaux Foundation in Devon, Pennsylvania, Ms. Hislop undertook graduate studies at California State University, Los Angeles, and completed her MA degree in 1986. During that period she worked with runaway teens in crisis and with substance-dependent adults in residential treatment.

Currently Ms. Hislop lives in Fresno, California, where she is completing doctoral studies in clinical psychology at the California School of Professional Psychology. There, she has recently worked as a therapist for abused youths and their families and for community college students. She is a part-time instructor at Fresno City College, where she teaches courses in psychology, human sexuality, and assertiveness training.

Contents

Introduction

Rejection is the feeling of being denied something that you want, particularly in relationships with other people. Although often painful, rejection is a normal part of being human. When you face it with a healthy attitude, it can be an excellent means of learning about your feelings and your values. At times rejection can provide motivation for positive self-development that otherwise might not occur.

Everyone has faced some form of rejection. An unfavorable response when applying for a job or for a position on a team is a form of rejection, as is a refusal of a date or a cold shoulder from someone you have considered a friend. Some people face rejection by becoming depressed or angry and letting those feelings overwhelm them. These people often have trouble moving forward and facing similar situations, or they create problems that make their situation worse. Others pay attention to their feelings about rejection but use them differently.

This book is designed to help you cope in a positive way with feelings that accompany rejection. We shall discuss identifying and taking care of feelings that get in the way of keeping an optimistic perspective. We shall examine how others have looked at their experiences of rejection and the steps they have taken to learn from them. We shall discuss when and how changes should be made to reduce rejection, and when and how to stay just as you are with your head held high. Finally, we shall discuss ways to interact with others to show your interest and confidence.

This book will not, however, attempt to help you eliminate rejection. People who have experienced rejection have put themselves into a situation where the outcome was uncertain. They took a chance! People who take chances despite the fact that rejection might occur often have the most fulfilling lives in the long run. Those people who keep a healthy attitude in the face of rejection are people who make things happen for themselves.

May you be one of them!

CHAPTER ◇ 1

Ouch!
Acknowledging
Feelings of Rejection

Rejection may result from a wide range of situations and involve many emotions. Rejection can be the feeling of sadness at the loss of a lover, the sting of humiliation from being cut from a team, or the disappointment of not getting a desired job or being accepted by a desired college. It can be anger at a friend who always seems to be busy when he or she is needed or does not follow through on plans that you have made together. Sometimes rejection can result from several separate situations, or it can create many emotions all mixed together.

Many of the emotions that can come with rejection are difficult to manage. Nonetheless, emotions are important when it comes to solving problems. Like physical pain, emotional pain tells you that a problem exists and can motivate you to find a solution. Consider the feelings that you have when you prick your finger. There is a sharp sting that is uncomfortable. Without that sting, however, you might not notice that your hand is in danger. Like physical feelings, emotions can let people know that a problem exists before they would otherwise recognize it. Having a healthy ability to experience emotions can help you to identify problems that can cause rejection or result from it. Recognizing a problem is a first step in finding a solution.

Losing your ability to feel emotions would in some ways be like losing your ability to experience physical sensations. Losing your ability to experience painful feelings, whether physical or emotional, could allow you to be hurt without feeling the sensations that motivate you to protect yourself and improve your situation. You might never learn to correct or to avoid painful situations because you would not be aware that they were harmful to you.

Rejection is usually painful. It may involve emotions ranging from sadness to anger to embarrassment. In learning to cope with rejection, people sometimes lose touch with their feelings and fail to notice what is bothering them. Imagine that you have been turned down for a date to an important dance and are feeling rejected. Now imagine that you don't bother to notice that your feelings are hurt. You tell yourself that you don't care about the person, the date, or the dance. In fact, you don't care about ever dating again. You don't ask anyone else to the dance, and you never again ask the would-be date out. Your feelings are completely ignored. The dance comes. The dance goes. You don't care. The problem of being turned down is never solved.

Painful feelings can be rough to experience after a brush with rejection. Emotions such as anger, sadness, or embarrassment are never easy to feel. Without them, however, you might never be aware of a need for change, or you might be aware of a need for change without feeling the emotional push to go about making it. Creating a plan to cope with rejection might have all of the emotional incentive of a math problem rather than being a challenge that emotionally compels you to take action. Specific feelings point to specific changes that need to be made and can provide incentive for making them happen.

People react differently when faced with the same experience of rejection. What makes one person sad might make another person angry. What might be embarrassing to one person might be humorous to another and infuriating to another. Understanding a specific emotional reaction to rejection can help to create a better understanding of a problem. If your emotional reaction to a friend with no time for you is disappointment, for instance, the problem might be what to do about a friend that you can't rely on. If your reaction to the same problem is embarrassment or humiliation, the problem might be finding a way to feel better about yourself. If your response is anger or fury, you may need to decide how to manage your temper effectively. To be able to use your feelings to help identify a problem, it is helpful to learn to recognize your emotions.

Learning to recognize your emotions in response to rejection requires paying close attention to your body sensations, your thoughts, and your behaviors. How you experience a particular emotion may be entirely different from the way another person experiences it, and the situations in which you experience an emotion might be entirely different from those in which another person experiences it. It is your own feelings that will help you decide how to handle a rejection. Recognizing feelings can help you to identify and address a problem before it gets out of hand.

Consider anger. In many situations of rejection you

may have this feeling. Perhaps someone has "pushed the buttons" that make you angry; someone was rude or insulting or did something that got you steamed up. Close your eyes and imagine how you would feel in such a situation. How would your body feel? What would you be thinking and saying to yourself? What would you be doing? Some of the physical sensations that might be associated with an angry response to rejection include muscle tension, an increased heart rate or breathing rate, twitching, shaking, or a flushed face. Behavior might include yelling, throwing a tantrum, clenching a fist, frowning, pacing, clenching your teeth, or glaring. Thoughts might include fantasies of revenge. By becoming able to identify the personal ways in which you experience anger, you become able to use this emotion as a guide.

Imagine the problems that could be faced by a person who is not aware of an angry response to rejection. Jill, for example, was a high school student who was frequently teased by her classmates. She pushed away her feelings of anger about the situation, however, by telling herself that it didn't matter, that they were only kidding. Eventually she lost any awareness of her anger. As you might guess, her situation at school never improved. Because she told herself that nothing was wrong, nothing needed to be improved. Because she did not pay attention to her feelings, she lost the desire to take action. She made no complaints to her teachers, no attempts to stand up for herself, and no efforts to avoid the students who were bothering her.

Sometimes problems can arise with the backfiring of plans to avoid an angry response to rejection. Rick's friends constantly backed out of their plans with him at the last minute. Rick acted as if that did not hurt him. He made no complaints to his friends, no suggestions for improvement, and no attempts to make new friends. He behaved as if his friends' actions didn't bother him in the least—that is, until he couldn't hold it in anymore and lost his temper in History class. Now he has two former friends and a reputation for having an explosive temper that is making it difficult to make new friends. Ignoring his anger created problems for him later.

Recognizing an angry response to rejection in its early stages can be important in managing it effectively. To better understand how you might experience this emotional reaction, consider how others have described their experiences with it:

Gus: When Coach kicked me off the team, I was so angry that my entire body tightened up. My shoulders hurt and started to shake. I was so hot and sweaty that a vein over my eyebrow started pounding. All I could think was, "I want to hit something!"

Pete: Once I was really bummed out about a class. It seemed that no matter what I did, I couldn't pass. When I tried to tell Mom about it, she was too busy to listen. I got really quiet, and my throat began to hurt. I started telling Mom off in my head.

Rosa: When I was rejected by my first-choice college, I wasn't sure that I would get in anywhere. I was real touchy that month, waiting to find out. The slightest little thing made me go off. My face kept getting all tight, and people said I looked really mean.

Sara Ellen: Once as a joke two guys pretended that they both liked me. When I asked them out, they both said no, for fun. At first I was a little miffed, but I shrugged it off. When I found out what was going on, though, I was so mad that I blanked out and couldn't think straight. I needed to get away before I made a scene.

Each of these descriptions of an angry response to rejection is probably a little different from your own. Maybe you recognize your anger by a tightness in your shoulders or a general feeling of being on edge, or by a sense of frustration or the desire to throw a temper tantrum. The point is that being aware of your anger is a first step in deciding what to do about it.

Sadness is another emotion that can accompany rejection. You feel disappointed or left out, unloved or unappreciated. As with anger, your sad response to rejection may be different from those of others. However, it is *your* emotions that count in making your decisions, not how others might feel or how you think you *should* feel.

Your feelings of sadness in response to rejection might include having less energy or not feeling good about yourself. Your mood might range from a mild sense of unhappiness to an all-out case of the blues or depression; from a slight ache of disappointment to an all-night crying session. As you think about how you feel, think, and act when sad about rejection, consider what you might have in common with the following people.

Paige: When my parents split up, Dad stopped coming around, and I felt rejected. After school I would come home and put on the saddest records I had. Sometimes it seemed as if every sad song I played was about me. It was hard to find things to feel good about.

Jasmine: When I didn't make the marching band tryouts, I felt as though everything about me was wrong. I couldn't stand how I looked, or my voice, or my friends, or my family, or the way I played my stupid saxophone. People started noticing that I was being rude.

Wes: When Pauline broke up with me, things were like Blah! Blah! Blah! Sadness can be like the whole world turns gray and you only hear monotones. I got really bored. The weirdest thing was that I couldn't fall asleep at night for thinking about how bored I was.

Tim: When I transferred schools I had a hard time making new friends. I was really trying to hang out with one group until I heard one of the girls say that I was a loser. That really hurt. It got hard to keep trying. I started spending a lot of time watching TV, and I lost most of my energy. It was hard to eat.

At times the emotions that come with rejection can be mixed. It is common, for instance, to have a response that is both sad and angry. A person who has hurt you may also have made you furious. You may alternate between two emotions or experience conflicting emotions at the same time. Sometimes people who have felt rejected by a particular person find themselves in the odd predicament of both loving and hating him or her at the same time. Sometimes identifying emotions so that you can deal with them involves teasing out two different emotions, or even three or four.

Among the emotions that can be tied in to rejection is a sense of embarrassment. You didn't get into a college that you had bragged about attending; you asked someone to dance at a party and were publicly insulted, or in the course of being rejected you were caught in a lie. Embarrassment is the feeling of being self-conscious, as if all eyes are upon you. Sometimes it involves shame or humiliation. Consider how others have described embarrassment in response to rejection

George: I remember going into the gym last term to see the list of who had been cast in the school play. I had been bragging all week that I had the lead role. When I found out that I only had a four-line part I was so embarrassed! My throat got dry and I couldn't talk. I kept thinking, "Damn, how stupid of me." Then I started to pray, "Please, God, let this be a dream; please let me wake up now." People kept asking me all week if I had the role I wanted. I didn't know what to say.

Candi: I always get picked last for teams because I'm an athletic flop. It's embarrassing. My friends tease me when I'm embarrassed because I start to giggle and can't stop. My stomach feels fluttery, and I feel weak. It's humiliating. I burn from my shoulders to my head. My ears get a tingly feeling. I want to become invisible.

Leon: I once asked a girl out, and she wouldn't even look at me. When I finally got the hint

and left, I realized that my zipper was wide
open. I hate being embarrassed! My one
thought is to cover it up, play it off! I lie,
I make up stories, I start talking real fast.
There was no way out of that one, though. I
hate that feeling.

Embarrassment, anger, and sadness are just some of the
emotional reactions that can come with rejection. Perhaps
"sad" does not describe your emotion in a particular situation as well as "forgotten," or "displeased," or "unhappy."
Perhaps "let down," "put down," or "devastated" are more
accurate for some situations than "embarrassed." Maybe
"anger" does not describe your emotion as well as "rage,"
or "annoyance," or "pestered." Sometimes finding the
right word to describe an emotion can be the first step in
understanding exactly what you feel during an unpleasant
situation. Human emotions are many, and it may take
some time to understand exactly what you are feeling.

An important emotional reaction to understand is stress.
Stress often can occur by itself. It is commonly mixed in
with other reactions such as sadness, anger, or embarrassment. Stress is the feeling of being tense, "wound up," or
anxious. Stress can occur under tense conditions—taking
an exam, for example, or performing for an audience; but it
can also be mixed with feelings that accompany rejection.

People describe stress reactions in response to rejection
in various ways. For some, it is an overall feeling of muscle
tension. Shoulders tense up, for example, or neck muscles
tighten. Some people feel their heart beating faster or their
breathing rate increase. Perhaps their mouth grows dry or
their palms get sweaty. Some people experience symptoms
such as stomach pain, diarrhea or constipation, rash, or
headache. For some, it is simply a feeling of being edgy

or worn out. Consider how the following people describe their stress reactions to rejection.

Denver: I once didn't get a job that I really needed. I started getting sick. I would get head-aches for no reason or throw up. I started losing sleep, and I worried a lot.

Lorraine: I once went to a party with some people I had just met. I got into an argument with one of the girls and thought that everyone would back me up, but they didn't. They just took off and left me alone at the party where I didn't know anyone. It was awful. I started breathing fast, and I could feel my heart pounding. My face turned red, and I was sweating. It was hard to concentrate on what to do next.

Chris: I get really motivated under stress. When the coach told me that I was going to be kicked off the team if I didn't bring my grades up, I turned things around fast. I knew that I needed to take charge and get things done. It was like I was being chased by an elephant.

Taylor: I was in a talent contest at school. After we had performed, we all lined up on stage, and they picked the winners in order. There were eight of us, and I came in last. I was so stressed out at not being the winner! My knees felt weak, and my throat got all dry. My mind just went blank.

Sometimes stress is the first reaction to rejection that you become aware of. You may have a general sense of feeling "not right," or "stressed out" before you are able

to pinpoint specifically what you are feeling. Identifying
a stress response to rejection can be a good first step in
recognizing the emotions that rejection has created.

Sometimes when people are struggling with difficult
emotional responses to rejection, they begin to feel hopeless. In an emotional state it is often hard to remember that
things usually get better, that painful emotions eventually
subside and you find ways to make things better.

That is especially true if you give in to a sense of hope-
lessness. One of the aspects of feeling hopeless is the
perception that nothing will ever get better. It is especially
important to recognize the emotional response of hopeless-
ness and to identify it as temporary. People have described
a hopeless response to rejection in the following ways:

Debbie: When all my friends left for college I wanted
to go away. I was desperate for a change, and
I felt empty, as if time was standing still.
Things didn't seem real.

Bertha: When I failed to make the basketball team, I
lost my faith. Everyone around me seemed
mean. I kept getting fed up with things. My
enthusiasm for life got lost, and no one could
cheer me up. It's like being a truck that has
run out of gas.

Larry: When my fiancé broke up with me to date
my friend, I felt as if no one cared about me;
if I had disappeared, no one would have
noticed. It felt like being water in a bathtub
when someone pulled the plug.

Experiencing painful emotions is useful in creating
change. That is not to suggest, however, that you act only

according to your emotions, or that you focus on your feelings to the point that you become stuck, or feel lost in them. Once you realize that you have pain, it is important not to ignore it, but to take appropriate steps to deal with the problem that is hurting you. As with physical pain, coping with emotional pain may require that you plan a solution, rather than acting on an initial impulse. If you feel a prick on your finger while in a doctor's office, for example, analysis of the situation may suggest a solution other than your initial impulse to pull your hand away. Taking care of yourself when you have painful feelings involves carefully thinking a situation through.

In learning to cope with rejection, it is important to be able to identify emotional reactions and to accept them as normal. Everyone faces problems, and everyone experiences rejection. The bad feelings that can come with rejection should be accepted and treated as messages that something is wrong. Once they are recognized and accepted, you can begin to take care of your emotions and to make the decisions that will improve your situation.

CHAPTER 2

Emotional First Aid

W hen rejection causes bad feelings, it is important to take care of them. Like a skinned knee or sprained ankle, hurt feelings require care to promote healing. Applying emotional first aid does not eliminate the source of the problem. Rather, it reduces emotional pain so that you can function. It's a bit like taking aspirin for a headache. Sometimes it is necessary to take care of strong feelings before it is possible to make good decisions about how to cope with the problems that are causing them.

Coping with rejection can be difficult. Emotional responses can become overwhelming and interfere with the ability to think clearly. Reactions of anger, sadness, embarrassment, or stress can interfere with the ability to function well and to handle rejection. Sometimes those emotions can be so upsetting that it is hard even to admit that they exist. Admitting having strong feelings is the first step in addressing them. Taking the time to deal with them is the second step.

Anger can be a normal reaction to rejection. Handled well, it can serve as motivation to take charge of and correct a troublesome situation. Handled badly, it can make complete chaos out of an already difficult problem. Losing control of anger can bring about disastrous results.

Let's take Rich, for example, who is rudely turned down for a date. Imagine that he handles his anger by throwing a tantrum. He throws his books through a window, calls the young woman a few colorful names, and stalks away feeling great—for about an hour. As his anger dies down, however, Rich begins to feel embarrassed at the scene he has made and guilty that the things he said may have hurt her. He begins to realize the impact that his anger will have on his life. He will be stuck with a huge bill to replace the window. In addition to being suspended from school, he will probably gain a bad reputation. In the end, of course, he still has no date and is not likely to get one any time soon. Rich is in trouble because he has not learned to manage his angry reaction.

Many people mismanage their angry responses to rejection because they view anger as a fighting emotion. They believe that when they are angry they need to fight, and they either do so or become intimidated and back away. Fighting, however, is only one of many ways to handle anger. Others can lead to more favorable outcomes. Taking time to acknowledge feelings and to cool them down can take the fight out of anger and allow good decisions to be made.

Taking time to leave an irritating situation and regroup is one of the simplest and most effective ways to cope with an angry response to rejection. It allows you to decide how to best take charge rather than simply reacting with blind emotion. If you have learned to recognize your symptoms of anger, you can leave as soon as you realize that you are beginning to get angry.

People go to all kinds of places to get away from situations involving rejection. Imagination is important. Locking yourself in a bathroom, going for a walk, hiding in a tree house, or going to your room are all options. The critical point is to get away from the situation until you have a plan for coping with it.

Sometimes this can work even better if you have a partner to help you. If anger is your typical reaction to rejection, have a partner around when you are taking risks that could involve being rejected. The partner can give you a signal when you are getting angry and need to leave. It should be someone who is likely to be around when a problem occurs: the classmate who sits with you at lunch, for example, when the obnoxious sophomore tries to shut you out of the conversation.

Sometimes partners are people who overreact to perceived rejection by each other. They might agree ahead of time to allow one partner to leave without question when a situation between them becomes tense. Two close friends or a boyfriend and girlfriend may work out such an agreement. Planning ahead for dealing with anger is a good idea, especially if it is a regular problem for you.

After an experience with rejection, several ways of releasing angry feelings work well. Physical outlets are useful for some people. Punching cushions, mattresses, or other soft objects can release angry tension. Sometimes breaking things can do the trick, if the objects are chosen carefully in advance. Eggs, for example, can be taken outside and smashed to bits with no harm done and at very little expense. Scrap paper or rags can be collected for shredding when an experience with rejection causes angry feelings.

Other forms of physical exertion can help to release angry tension. Exercising or working out can help to blow off steam. Going for a walk or a run can help. Many people let out their aggression on a tennis or volleyball court or by playing baseball or basketball.

After a brush with rejection, some people burn off anger with physical activities around the house. Vigorously polishing furniture, washing walls, rearranging closet space can provide a good workout. In the same way, outdoor work such as leaf-raking, hedge-trimming, and weeding can help to release anger.

When hostility is felt toward a particular person, acting out aggression on a substitute object can be helpful. For example, draw a picture of the person who rejected you and then tear it up, yell at it, squirt it with a water pistol, or run over it with a bicycle. Variations on this theme can be performed with photographs, clay models, or paper dolls.

Writing a letter to the person involved can release angry feelings. It can contain all of your angriest, ugliest thoughts and wishes. The letter does not have to be sent. When it's finished, it can be ripped into shreds as a further release.

If nothing else works, finding an isolated place and screaming at the top of your lungs may do it. Sometimes a good cry can be in order. Anger is a normal emotion that often accompanies rejection. Taking the time to acknowledge and release excessive anger can help you to cope effectively with the situation that is causing it.

Sadness, like anger, can cause problems when it is allowed to become overwhelming or when it is ignored. Consider Sally, who is not invited to a party and who feels rejected. She becomes very sad and begins to spend time alone. She overeats and neglects her health and her daily activities. Well after the party has come and gone, Sally is still spending most of her time alone in her room feeling sad and doing nothing to change her mood. Before long her depression keeps her from going out at all. Because she does not take care of her feelings, they eventually get the best of her.

Like anger, sadness should be attended to following an experience of rejection so that it does not interfere with the ability to make good decisions. Sometimes people like to be alone when feeling sad and rejected. Solitary time can be comforting in small doses. Ramon, a college freshman, explains his use of solitude as follows: "When I was rejected by my first-choice college, I just didn't feel like being good company. Hanging out with the guys was making me feel antisocial, and I wasn't ready to talk about what was bothering me. I went home and took off on a long walk with my dog Bob. At times like that, I swear he's the only one that understands me. I told him how bad I felt and how disappointed I thought my family would be, not to mention how disappointed I was with myself."

"The next day after school, Bob and I stayed in my room. Bob didn't say too much. He just sat there and let me hug him. I thought a lot about what I was going to say to every-one, and about what I would do if my second-choice school didn't come through. Sometimes I need to be alone like that to think things out. I don't mind if Bob's there though. He's a good listener, and if I need to cry he doesn't tell anyone." Time alone can help you to sort out your thoughts and feelings. Take care, though, if you find yourself spending more than a couple of days on your own. Too much time alone can make you feel lonely on top of being sad.

Be good to yourself when you are feeling rejected. It is important to remain friendly with yourself even when others do not. You can be your own best friend for a while. Think about your favorite things to do and do them. Nurture yourself. Give yourself a bubble bath. Make yourself tea. Be sure that you eat right. Give yourself some kind words and a present. Take yourself out.

For about a dollar you can buy yourself a small treat: a flower, ice cream, an arcade game or two, a tropical fruit, a comic book, a new cosmetic, a dimestore toy, a hamburger, an exotic tea sample. With a little imagination, a dollar or so can be stretched into a lot of good cheer.

Using creativity can sometimes turn the blues around. Expressing feelings by keeping a journal or by writing poetry can help. Activities such as dancing, drawing, painting, woodshop, gardening, knitting can turn sad feelings into creative energy.

Exercise is also an excellent way to chase away the blues. Vigorous physical activity can make you feel invigorated and alive. It is hard to feel down when your blood is pounding through your body and all of your senses feel alert. A brisk walk is one of the easiest ways to exercise and is a great pick-me-up.

Taking extra care of your appearance can also serve as a pick-me-up. Take a shower, use your favorite makeup or after-shave, and wear your favorite outfit. Have your hair cut, or try styling it differently. It is hard to feel bad about someone's negative reaction to you when the person in the mirror looks ready to take on the world.

Sometimes, however, when people are hurting they simply need to cry. Rejection can sting. Crying is a natural emotional and physical release of bad feelings. It is something that almost everyone does when feeling sad.

Crying is difficult for some people, especially those who have been taught that it is a sign of weakness. The fact is, of course, that everyone is weak sometimes. For some people crying is a source of strength, in that it allows them to release the feelings that are interfering with their ability to take charge of themselves.

People who don't admit that they cry sometimes weep privately: at night, in the shower, or alone in their room.

They miss out on gaining comfort from others, of course. However, if the thought of shedding a tear makes you doubt your masculinity, crying in private might be a welcome release for you. Crying and sadness are natural reactions to a painful situation.

Rejection may be accompanied by stress or embarrassment. These emotions are also normal. They may be mixed with other feelings and difficult to sort out. During times of stress, muscles often feel tight and tense. Exercise can help you to relax. For tension in the shoulder area, try rolling your shoulders in a circle. For tension in the neck, gently drop your head forward and roll it in a slow half circle, then drop it backward for another half-circle roll. For other stress reduction exercises, check your school or public library for books on the subject. Stress reduction tapes that focus on muscle relaxation are also available.

Actively practicing relaxation can help you to get a handle on stress. One way to practice relaxation is to find a quiet spot and close your eyes. Focus on a gentle, calming thought. It might be a sound such as your own breathing or heartbeat, or a word that you find soothing such as "calm" or "relax." Use this word or sound to take the place of anxiety-producing thoughts; let them all slip away. If they try to sneak in, simply continue to focus on your calm thoughts until they disappear. If you find that this exercise works well for you, check your library for books or tapes on relaxation or on meditation.

Imagination can be an excellent tool for coping with the emotions brought about by rejection. Picture yourself in a peaceful setting: resting on a beach, swinging in the park, even slouched in a big overstuffed chair. Try to picture clearly everything about your scene that makes it peaceful. Try to feel a gentle breeze, for example, or the warm sun on your face. Hear water lapping against the shore, or see kites sailing overhead. Be creative! In a few minutes your bad feelings should begin to ease away.

Imagination can be a powerful tool when a stress response first hits. Immediately following a negative experience, picture the rejecting person wearing boxer shorts or a pink bow tie. Seeing the person in a comical situation can take the impact out of rejection. This general idea can be used in a variety of situations when fear of rejection is getting in the way of your taking a chance. The person that you are afraid to ask out can be pictured as a teddy bear. The coworker that you are trying to approach about improving your working relationship can be pictured as having a gigantic wart on his nose.

Whenever you are having an emotional response to rejection, it is important to take extra care of your health. Being rundown physically can compound the problem. Some people encounter a vicious circle during emotional periods in their lives. They feel too upset to take care of themselves and become physically worn down. That causes them to feel worse emotionally and they neglect themselves further, and so on.

People neglect themselves by overeating, or by undereating, or by neglecting to eat healthful foods. Take extra care to stick with proper foods during emotional times. Exercise is also important, both for managing emotions and for staying healthy. Remember that a new exercise program should be started slowly and with a doctor's okay. Exercise plans tend to work best when they are fun and easy to fit into your schedule.

Rest is important during emotional times. If you have trouble falling asleep, practice relaxing before bedtime. Be sure that you are comfortable in your sleeping quarters. Avoid caffeine, which is found in coffee, tea, colas, and diet pills. Avoid using sleeping pills without consulting your doctor, as regular use can actually contribute to restlessness. Instead, try a warm bath or shower, or a warm drink such as hot milk or herbal tea. Read a very dull book until you find yourself becoming drowsy.

It is wise to avoid the use of over-the-counter drugs, alcohol, and cigarettes during emotional times, as it may be very tempting to overuse them. It is also common sense not to abuse your body with these substances when you are physically or emotionally run down, when your body may have less energy to clean up after them.

When going through an experience with rejection, consider talking to someone. The person can be anyone you trust—a teacher, a friend, a phone counselor, a doctor, coach, relative. If your emotions ever lead you to consider harming yourself, talking to someone is a *must*! If you find yourself thinking of suicide or any other kind of self-injury, contact your hospital, police, or mental health center. For almost everyone, suicidal feelings are temporary and pass eventually if proper care is taken.

Many people consult with a mental health counselor when they are having to cope with strong emotional responses to rejection. In counseling, people work with a trained professional to explore their thoughts, feelings, and behaviors. Counselors have different ideas about what is important in this process. If you choose to work with a counselor, you should ask his or her opinions on the matter and be sure that you are comfortable both with the counselor and with his or her recommendations.

A school counselor or family physician can refer you to a counselor. The phone book may have counselors listed under "Mental Health," "Psychologists," or "Social Workers." You might also look in the emergency section of the phone book for a crisis hotline or referral network.

Everyone at one time or another is faced with strong

emotions stemming from a rejection. Anger, sadness, stress, and embarrassment are just a few of the normal emotions that such an experience can produce. Ignoring such emotions does not make them go away. Allowing them to be blown out of proportion can interfere with your ability to address the problems that are causing them. Paying attention to strong emotions is a crucial first step in addressing a painful rejection.

CHAPTER ◇ 3

Express Yourself!

C oping with problems often requires the ability to speak up and express yourself. Learning to express yourself can help others get to know you. It allows you to connect with others to let them know that you need help in coping with rejection or that you are having a problem with something they are doing. It allows you to correct a problem or a misunderstanding in a relationship before rejection ensues. If part of your plan for coping with rejection is to reach out to others for help, or to make new friends, or to clear up the problems that have led to rejection, learning to express yourself is crucial.

One of the simplest but most important ways to help others to know and understand you is to use the word "I" often. Let your opinions and ideas be important! When you use the word "I" in a sentence, you let someone else get to know you a little better. Think of the possibilities, for example, when you find ways to fill in the blanks of sentences: "I think _____," "I like _____.," "I want you to know that _____." Dozens of opportunities arise each day to express an opinion or an idea that will help other people to understand you.

To be able to express yourself, you must believe that what you have to say counts. And why wouldn't it? Think for a moment how you feel when you are confused about what someone is thinking. Do you prefer to be kept in the dark, or to understand the person? You probably prefer to have a clear idea of where you stand in relation to that person. Similarly, others will prefer to know what is happening with you. Letting people know you allows them to find things to like about you. It helps them to know when you have a problem with which you need help. It bridges silence that can lead to rejection.

Sometimes you can let another person know you by helping him or her to understand your emotions—using the words "I feel. . ." That is easy when your feelings are positive. You exclaim, "I feel terrific," or "I feel like dancing." It's fun to share a good mood. If the idea of sharing feelings is new to you, this can be a good place to start.

One way to begin sharing your feelings is to erase the word "fine" from your vocabulary, especially in response to the question, "How are you?" Instead, choose a word that more accurately describes your feelings and add a sentence or two explaining them. "I feel great," for example, "the home team won again," or "I'm not at my best, actually. I have some things on my mind."

Some feelings are easy to share. More difficult to share are the kinds of feelings that can come with rejection. Anger, for example, or sadness may not bring the same kind of positive reactions from others. Often people feel vulnerable or afraid to share these emotions. They worry about what others may think or that others may not be interested.

Some people envisage disaster if they share their less pleasant emotions. "If I tell him I'm angry, he will hate me and turn all of my friends against me." "If I tell her that I am sad, she'll laugh in my face and call me a loser. I'll be humiliated." "If I say I'm embarrassed, my life will be ruined." Many people build up unrealistic fears of the reactions that others will have to their unpleasant emotions.

Often people are pleasantly surprised by the results of sharing their emotions. Discussing how you feel can help to clarify your emotions. Voicing your emotions can also be a great relief for the person listening to you. Your listener may already suspect that you are struggling with a difficult emotion but have no idea what it is. If the problem involves her or him, expressing yourself opens the door to finding a solution. Giving your feelings to another person may bring support, encouragement, or useful advice. Often a person who is aware of your feelings will choose to share his or her own feelings with you. You send the message that it is okay for the two of you to talk about personal things and allow a close friendship to develop.

Of course it is always possible that you won't get positive results when you share your feelings with another person. Some people are insensitive, unfeeling, or simply don't know what to do when others share their feelings. Sharing uncomfortable feelings is always a risk and may be scary. Unfortunately, some people allow their fear of other people's reactions to rule them. They never share their unhappy or unpleasant emotions. Although they never have to be concerned about other people's reactions, they also never enjoy the benefits that come with sharing or working out feelings with another person.

Sometimes it can be hard to know whom to talk to, or whether the person you choose will understand. Trusting another person involves risk. There is no easy way to predict the reactions. There are some guidelines, however, to making such a decision. You may know someone—a classmate, a teammate, a teacher, a coach, a friend's parent, a counselor, a coworker—who has a reputation as a good listener or of being able to keep secrets. You may know someone whom you feel good about or believe to be trustworthy. These can be good people to risk sharing feelings with.

Of course, one of the best ways to find out if someone is willing to talk about personal feelings is to ask. Asking if someone is willing to listen and has the time is a way to test the waters. It lets you take the small risk of revealing that something is bothering you without taking the larger risk of revealing what that something is. This can prevent your revealing more vulnerable emotions to someone not willing or able to respond. Questions to ask to find out if someone is willing to listen to a problem related to rejection might sound like one of these:

- I need to talk to someone; are you free?
- I have something personal that's bothering me. Can I talk to you after class?
- I need to get something off my chest. Is there a time when we can talk?

If the person shows a willingness to hear you out, you have the option of expressing yourself on a more personal level.

When discussing feelings with others, it can be helpful for them to know what you need or would like from them. Some people find it hard to ask for that kind of help because they don't know what to say. If you are new to expressing your feelings or asking for help, try filling in the blanks of this simple formula, "I'm feeling _____ and I'd like _____."

For example:

- I'm feeling down, and I'd like to hear some of your jokes.
- I'm feeling bad about an argument I had with my girlfriend, and I'd like your opinion about what to do now.
- I'm feeling put down by my math teacher, and I'd like it if you would listen while I blow off steam for a while.
- I'm embarrassed about messing up a science problem in front of the class, and I'd like to know if you have ever had a class make fun of you.

Making such requests is never a guarantee that they will be granted. It gives the other person a clue, however, as to how to help you. A negative response may mean that you need to try again, or it may be a clear indication that the person is unable to help. If you are not sure what a response means, you can—ask! Sometimes it takes effort to be understood and helped.

The need to share feelings related to rejection can be a direct result of the effects of someone's actions on you. A person's actions can make you feel rejected or experience any of the many emotions that can go with rejection. Occasionally this will be done on purpose. Some people feel powerful or superior by being rejecting of others or putting them down. In many cases, however, people honestly don't realize how their actions affect others.

When someone's actions bother you, you can say so. In that way you let him or her know (and remind yourself) that your feelings are important, that you are worthy of respect. You also do the person a courtesy by informing him of the effects of his behavior on you. This gives him or her the option to change the behavior or to discuss the matter. For some people, such information may be helpful to their other relationships. It may well be that the actions that disturb you have had similar effects on other people, and your feedback may enable the person to understand and improve other relationships.

Such feedback is usually best received if given in a respectful manner. Be specific about what the other person does that bothers you or makes you feel rejected. Describe only what you can *see* or *hear*, and refrain from judging the behavior or guessing at the motivation behind it. Then describe your own emotions in response. Putting these two ideas together, you may come up with sentences similar to the following:

- "When you don't return my phone calls [you can hear this], I feel hurt." (Rather than: "You don't care about me!")
- "When you walk down the hall with your boyfriend everyday after classes [you can see this], I feel left out. (Rather than: "You're getting really stuck up since you met Jim.")
- "When you told Ann that my dress made me look like a rag doll [you can hear this], I felt angry!" Rather than: "Jerk!"

When you limit your information to a description of a behavior and your emotional reaction to it, you avoid criticizing or judging the other person. Most people react negatively to being criticized or judged. Merely describing actions and reactions keeps name-calling, insults, and put-downs out of the picture. It also avoids assumptions about the person's motives. No one can know for sure what someone else is thinking. If you try, you may find yourself in a no-win debate over intent rather than addressing the real issue of how you were affected.

Consider how that might occur:

You: "DeeAnn, it bothers me how you're always trying to make me look dumb."

DeeAnn: "I don't try to make you look dumb. You're too sensitive."

You: "I am not. You were trying to make me look stupid!"

DeeAnn: "I made a few jokes. I was not trying to put you down!"

You: "You were too!"

DeeAnn: "Was not. See ya!"

Note that the real issue of your feeling put down or rejected is never addressed. Note also that DeeAnn is never given a clear explanation of what she has done that was offensive. She has no idea what specific things are putting you off. She seems to be irritated with your criticism, and the argument over what she *meant* to do could go on until next week without your ever being sure of her intentions.

Consider how the conversation might go with more specific feedback limited to her behavior and your feelings in reaction to it.

You: "When you said I couldn't add five and six without taking off my shoes to count on my toes, I felt put down."

DeeAnn: "I was only making a joke. You're too sensitive."

You: "I don't think I'm too sensitive. When you made that joke, I felt hurt."

DeeAnn: "Sorry. I guess I just won't joke around with you any more."

You: "I like it when you joke around sometimes.

I was tickled when you joked about how we used to sneak out of gym class and watch the guys do push-ups from under the bleachers. But when you make jokes about my math ability, I feel hurt."

DeeAnn: "That could make sense. Okay, sorry!"

When you share feelings with people, it is sometimes appropriate to request a change in behavior: "I would like you to stop making jokes at my expense." The requested change should focus only on a behavior that you can see or hear, to avoid judging or second-guessing intentions.

If a request is especially important to you, or if you feel that you have not been heard, you can state what your reaction will be if your request is not followed. "If you do not stop, I will no longer want to spend time with you," or, "If you continue to make jokes at my expense, I will no longer consider you my friend." Be sure that your statement of what might happen is accurate and does not come across as an idle threat. Consider how you might combine giving specific, nonjudgmental feedback along with a request for change in the following examples:

- When you tell me to shut up, I feel annoyed. I would like you to listen to what I have to say. (If you do not care to listen, I will not want to continue this conversation with you.)
- When you say that I am not qualified for this job, I think you may have overlooked my coursework in business school. I would appreciate your reviewing it. (If you decide not to review it, I think you'll be missing out on an excellent employee.)
- When you drank all those beers at the party and started telling dirty jokes to my boss, I was angry

and embarrassed. I would like you to limit your drinking when you are out with me. (Otherwise I'll go alone or take someone else to functions that are important to me.)

To be taken seriously when you express yourself, keep in mind several points. Standing up straight and looking a person in the eye (or at least in the face) conveys that you are confident about what you have to say. A strong, confident voice lets people know that you are to be taken seriously. Raising your chin about a half inch and putting your shoulders back by about the same amount gives you a confident posture.

Take care to avoid suggestions that your opinions are silly or trivial. Punctuating your conversation with phrases such as "just kidding," "not really," or "but that's only my opinion," reduces its effectiveness. Giggling reduces your ability to express the seriousness of your ideas, thoughts, or feelings.

Expressing yourself is always easiest when you keep the focus on yourself and allow your feelings, thoughts, and ideas to be important. It is easier still when you respect yourself as well as the person with whom you are speaking. It can take time and practice, but speaking up can go a long way in coping with a feeling of rejection and in resolving the misunderstandings that can lead to it.

CHAPTER ◇ 4

Talking to Yourself

I magine that you have been rejected, perhaps by a new acquaintance who has flatly stated that he no longer wishes to spend time with you. How will you explain to yourself what has happened? If you have had this kind of difficulty in the past, perhaps you have explained the occurrence in one of the following ways.

At one extreme you might have told yourself that it was no big deal. It was no skin off your nose. You couldn't care less. With this method of coping, feelings are pushed aside and the event is buried without examination. There is no opportunity to explore what went wrong. If a mistake was made on your part there is a good chance that it will be made again.

At the other extreme you may tend to take all the responsibility and give yourself a good chewing out. "Oh, I was so stupid! I should have.... I could have.... Everyone hates me. My life is ruined." In this style of coping, thoughts are used to influence feelings by blowing them out of proportion.

Many psychologists believe that what you say to yourself about a problem influences your feelings. When your emotions are bruised from a brush with rejection, what you say to yourself can help you to heal or can add self-inflicted damage to already hurt feelings.

There are several ways to chew yourself out after you have been rejected. One way is to assume that something is "wrong" with you or that *many* things are wrong with you. You examine your personality, your hair, your face, your clothes, your body, your speech, your car, your manners, your teeth! Like a slide under a microscope, your faults are blown up and scrutinized. Generally if you examine yourself this closely you will find something that could use improvement and that can "explain" why you were rejected: "Of course s/he rejected me, my hair is too messy." "My tush is too big." "My legs are bony." "I can't do math."

On the plus side, this kind of self-criticism can take the uncertainty out of the experience. If you find a reason for having been rejected, you no longer have to feel confused about what happened. There can be an odd security in "knowing" that you are to blame. It may be of more comfort to have a self-depreciating explanation than no explanation at all.

The down sides are obvious, however. When you magnify your faults it is easy to become upset or saddened, which adds to an already difficult experience. If you automatically attribute rejection to your faults, you will often be wrong. Jumping to such conclusions can keep you from understanding what really happened and from learning from it. You can wind up more upset over your "faults" than over the rejection itself and still have no better understanding of what went on.

If you find something about yourself that you feel is undesirable, you can go a step further and decide that *everything* about you is wrong. You identify an awkward moment in a conversation when it appeared that you offended another person and use that single incident as evidence that you are socially inept and incapable of ever being accepted. You meet someone who does not like your hairstyle and tell yourself that you are hopelessly ugly and unfashionable. Someone gives you what appears to be a disapproving stare when you wear your new outfit, and you decide that not only is it ugly but that you have no sense of style. By the time you finish talking to yourself, even *you* don't like yourself.

Being rejected does not mean that something is wrong with you. Perhaps that point seems obvious. People and their situations are infinitely different. Different people, different employers, different colleges, different sports teams all may have directly conflicting preferences as to whom they will accept as a friend, lover, employee, student, team player. A college may need science students, whereas you are good at management. A lover may want a wife while you want a casual relationship. A friend may find his niche in the theater, while you prefer bridge. Often what is interpreted as rejection or not being "good enough" is simply not fitting into a place that is not your style.

When feeling bad about a rejection, an appropriate question to ask yourself is, "Did I really want to be accepted here?" For example, Mary did not make the final cut for her school's marching band and is very disappointed. However, she hated practicing and did not attend all re-hearsals. Should she call herself a failure and agonize over not fitting in, or should she accept that she is not currently inclined to be a musician and retain her self-confidence? If Luis is turned down for a date because Lucy doesn't want to go with someone who is not a member of her church, should he put himself down because of his religious beliefs or decide that dating a girl with a closed mind would be uncomfortable? Should Nancy, who was excluded from a clique because she can't afford the "right" clothes, tell herself to feel bad about herself and her wardrobe or good about not hanging around a bunch of snooty kids? Often rejection is an opportunity to reexamine where you really want to fit in, and to tell yourself to like who you really are.

A few people, of course, take pleasure in rejecting others. It is a way to boost a low self-image or to feel important. Some feel that they have to reject even people that they like in order to fit in with some group. Some are just plain mean. When dealing with people of this sort, important questions to ask yourself are, "Would I really want to fit in here?" and "Am I going to let this type of person make me feel bad?" Do you choose to give such a person power over your mood and self-image, or do you choose to see him or her as a person with a problem?

Vanessa is walking down the hall at school with her girl-friend when Joe Popularity stops them. Ignoring Vanessa, he invites her friend to a party. When Vanessa asks if she might come, Joe looks down his nose at her, says, "Uh—I don't think so," and walks haughtily away. Should Vanessa let a guy like Joe ruin her day and her self-image? Or should she choose to view him as having an ego problem and bad manners and tell herself that she is better off not knowing him? When an emotional response to a person or situation is rejection and being put-down, often the problem is with the other person. Recognizing this and choosing not to let such a person dictate your mood or your opinion of yourself can help you in a difficult situation. Reminding yourself that you are okay can help you to *feel* okay.

Some people have trouble differentiating the signs of acceptance and rejection. When in doubt they find re-jection that never existed. Given an unclear situation, they tell themselves that they have blown it. Some people even invite rejection because, in spite of themselves, it is what they are most comfortable with. For example, when faced with a new situation—dating, interviewing for a job—a sign of impending rejection can reduce tension and anxiety by providing a possible way out. Larry wants to invite Maria out but is afraid he will make a fool of himself, have nothing to say, and totally turn her off. He plays a game with himself, and with Maria:

> "Maria, I want to ask you something, but you probably don't want to hear it."
> "What is it?"
> "I was gonna ask you to do something, but you might not want to do it."
> "Larry, if it's what I think it is, I'm not interested. I'm late for class."
> "Okay, see ya."

Larry leaves, relieved that he no longer has to worry about what to say on the date, but feeling rejected and hurt. Maria may be dying to go out with him but afraid that he was going to ask her to do his science homework (again!), or to skip class with him, or any number of things. In telling himself that Maria rejected him for a date, Larry may have been wrong. He might have done well to pause and ask himself whether he was sure that Maria's responses meant that she was not interested in him. He might also have done well to look at his own attitude. Larry entered the situation telling himself that Maria would never go out with him. He approached her with the thought, "I am someone you'll probably want to reject, so go ahead and do it." His presentation practically invited Maria to turn him down.

Larry had been turned down previously by a girl he had

wanted to date. Because of his fear that it would happen again, he was nervous about saying directly what he wanted. He had taken a single previous rejection to suggest to himself that he was unworthy as a date. He began acting like an "unworthy date." If he continues to think of himself and to act in this way, he may soon find that more people begin to treat him as unworthy—and who wants to go out with an "unworthy date"?

Some people find themselves locked into a vicious circle. They are rejected. They put themselves down. They feel bad. They lose self-confidence. They fail to present themselves well. They expect rejection. They are rejected, and so on.

Imagine that Larry does find a fault with himself. He overhears Maria telling her girlfriend that he had tried to ask her out but she had avoided him because his nose was too big. And it is! What should Larry tell himself? That he'll never get a date because of his nose? That he is terminally ugly and unworthy and should stop trying? Or should he reassure himself that his nose *is* rather grand but that no one is perfect.

Discovering that you are not perfect does not mean that you must feel bad about it, even if the flaw has led someone to reject you. If it did, most people would be walking around in serious states of depression. Rather than saying to yourself, "I have a flaw, so I must therefore feel bad," it is equally valid to tell yourself, "I have a flaw so I must be human," or, "My flaw makes me more interesting," or, "Others will feel more comfortable with me because I won't intimidate them by being perfect."

Of course, you may find something in yourself that you believe truly deserves feeling bad about. Perhaps you have hurt someone's feelings. Maybe you have a drug problem or an anger management problem. Having chosen to feel bad about a particular shortcoming does not mean that you must feeling bad about your entire self. It is possible to feel bad about a shortcoming and plan to improve it, while at the same time feeling good about your good points.

In exploring what to tell yourself about an experience with rejection, it can be useful to keep the following points in mind:

- Discovering that you may have contributed to an experience with rejection is not something to spend too much time feeling bad about. It is something to learn from. Remind yourself that no matter what you learn, you are basically an okay person.
- The crucial question to ask yourself when evaluating an experience with rejection is not, "What did I do wrong?"—which leads to self put-downs—but, "What (if anything) might I have done better?"— which focuses on things that you might improve.
- It takes two people to create a bad experience between two people. In addition to examining your role, remind yourself to consider what part the other person might have played. Tell yourself that looking for what you did "wrong" is not the only way to gain a better understanding of the experience.

Be careful how you talk to yourself after a brush with rejection. That can have a great impact on the outcome of the experience. Consider how this works for Marv, who invites his teammate Ron out for a soda after a ball game. Ron says he'd just as soon not go because, frankly, he finds Marv dull. Marv says to himself, "There is something terribly wrong with me—I am dull." He then sets out to prove it to himself by reviewing every time he ever told a bad joke. He remembers a time a month ago when he was turned down for a date and tells himself that it was because of his dullness. He ponders the time in third grade when he was not invited to a classmate's party and tells himself that this too was because of his lackluster personality.

Marv becomes very self-conscious about his "dullness" and begins to watch his every move. It becomes awkward to monitor himself and carry on conversations at the same time, and he begins to feel uncomfortable in social situations. He decides that what he must do is become exciting, and he begins to lie about himself in order to look good. As time goes on he becomes increasingly isolated from his friends and from people in general.

How might Marv have reacted differently? What else could he have said to himself following his experience with Ron? Keeping in mind the points mentioned above, he could recreate his "conversation" with himself. He might remind himself that he is an okay guy. He might remember that he is a good team player, a devoted and loyal friend, a fairly bright and attractive guy, and a monster third baseman.

He might then ask himself if there was anything that he could have done better. He might remember a couple of jokes that he told Ron that could have been considered a little dull and decide not to share his humor with Ron anymore. He might discover that he has not been hanging out with the guys as much as he had thought, or that he had recently forgotten to go to Ron's party.

Having looked at his part, Marv might then begin looking at Ron's contribution to their interaction. He might come to realize that Ron has an odd sense of humor and was only kidding. He may discover that Ron was under a good deal of stress that day and was snapping at everyone. He may simply conclude that Ron is a jerk who has a tendency to disregard the feelings of others.

After all this, Marv may tell himself something like this: "Hey, I'm an okay guy and I'm not going to let this get me down. Sure, I have an occasional episode of dullness—maybe I can start hanging out with the guys more often and stop telling the joke about the chicken in the gorilla suit—but overall I'm a pretty worthwhile person. I think Ron had a bad day. I'll give him the benefit of the doubt. If he keeps on with the put-downs, though, I'll have to rethink whether I want to associate with him."

Being rejected does not mean that something is wrong with you. Finding something about yourself that could be better does not mean that you have to feel bad. Choosing to feel bad about an honest flaw or mistake does not mean that you have to consider yourself an overall failure. Sometimes a situation that seems to involve rejection is really a matter of misinterpretation caused by things that you said to yourself. These ideas may seem obvious, but they are sometimes hard to remember when talking to yourself about rejection.

Consider the experience of Barbara, who is not elected to a student government post for which she was nominated and is feeling rejected by her peers. She tells herself that she must be a real deadbeat. She is embarrassed to be seen around the campus, telling herself that people must be talking about her. She begins cutting classes. Her grades drop, and she becomes ineligible for the next year's elections. She tells herself that she's a failure and begins to act like one. Before long, people begin to think less of her. How could Barbara have changed what she said to herself to create a better outcome?

Alternatively, Barbara might have reminded herself that her experience was an opportunity for learning. After all, she now has campaign experience that few others in her class possess. She has learned to give speeches with confidence, to organize her time, and to delegate tasks to her committee. She might have told herself that she was smart to run in the election, even if she did not win. In assessing what she might have done better, she might realize that she did not get her campaign under way quickly enough. Maybe she will decide that she was not experienced enough to gain the vote, or that she did not address issues with which the student body was concerned.

Barbara may choose to assess the ways in which the student body contributed to her experience. Perhaps they were concerned about scholarships while she was more interested in quality academics. Maybe her peers wanted more parties or more control over teacher evaluations. Perhaps they did not recognize a hard worker when they saw one. She can evaluate all of these possibilities in deciding what to tell herself.

Ultimately, Barbara might tell herself something like this: "I ran a good campaign. To win, though, I'd need to start a month earlier and to address the issue of having a big Homecoming party right after the first football game when everyone is excited for it. I'll also need to cater to the students' concern for a better teacher evaluation process. I think I'll talk it over with my campaign managers, and if they're willing, I'll try again next year!"

An experience with rejection can be hard to go through. It can be made better or worse by the way you treat yourself when it is over. If you choose to respond by reminding yourself of all of your faults and how they make you "inadequate," you can make a bad experience worse. If you remind yourself that you're an okay person, in spite of any areas that can use improvement, you can improve your chances of creating a favorable outcome.

The next time things go wrong, don't chew yourself out; sit yourself down and have a nice, supportive chat. Be on *your* side—you'll find that you like yourself a lot better.

CHAPTER ◇ 5

Why Me? And What Should I Do Now?

R ejection, no matter how painful, is always an opportunity for learning and self-improvement. It enables you to ask, "Why did this happen?" and "What, if anything, should I do now?" Answers to these questions can provide directions for self-development and change. Failure to ask these questions can lead to missed opportunities for moving forward and making worthwhile adjustments.

Often your immediate responses to these questions do not provide you with accurate information. They may be produced while you are in the midst of a difficult situation and based more on emotion than on fact. An initial reaction after being turned down for a date, for instance, might be to say to yourself, "He turned me down because I'm not attractive enough. I should never ask anyone out again," or "She turned me down because she thinks she's too good for everyone. I should find a way to take her down a notch." Taking time to examine what has happened may bring you

43

to realize that your immediate explanations were not entirely on target.

Taking time to reflect may also help you to consider possibilities other than your initial explanation. The would-be date may have a serious relationship, for example, or be pursuing one. He or she may have other previously made plans. Perhaps he or she simply perceives you as having dissimilar interests and (accurately or not) feels that you would not hit it off. Perhaps the would-be date is broke and would be embarrassed to have you pay for the evening. Maybe a recent relationship has soured the person on dating. Maybe he or she really meant that you're a wonderful person but an evening of classical music would be boring.

To get a better perspective on what has happened and what should be done, it is useful to consider other alternatives. Two possibilities for developing these alternatives are brainstorming and getting outside opinions.

Brainstorming is a rapid-fire listing of ideas without regard to logic. In brainstorming to consider possible reasons for rejection, let your mind wander and be creative. Write down everything that comes to mind, no matter how bizarre or unlikely. Ideas that seem the most unlikely at first may be right on target or can stimulate more reasonable possibilities. After brainstorming the ideas can be evaluated for their usefulness.

An example of brainstorming was created by Tim when he was cut from the basketball team:

Possible reasons the coach cut me from the team:
• Coach is a muffinhead.
• Coach plays favorites.
• Slow reactions.
• Poor shooting.

- Can't play defense.
- Don't cheer for the team when we are losing.
- Late to practice.
- Don't pay attention at practice.
- Told the coach to eat my gym shoes.
- Can't pass.
- Coach is secretly blind!

When Tim sits down to review his list, he will probably cross off most of the items having to do with skill. He's pretty quick and can play all positions about as well as most of the guys on the team. When he looks at the left-over items, however, it may occur to him for the first time that he did a lot of things that might have added up to a "bad attitude" in the coach's eyes. The items that he has listed may lead him to remember other things that could confirm this possibility: He *was* absent from a scrimmage, and he *did* miss two games last year.

Whereas his first thoughts about why he was being cut from the team had to do with the ignorance of his coach, Tim now has an idea that he can work with. It may come in handy when he next tries out for a team; he may even find other areas of his life where it has application. At any rate, taking the time to brainstorm ideas about his situation allowed Tim to learn something about himself that may be useful in preventing future rejections.

Tim might also have gained insight into the reasons for his being cut by asking for feedback from other team members. Sometimes other people are able to see things that you can't. Most of the team members had seen the coach's looks of frustration when dealing with Tim. They had also been at a practice (which Tim had missed) where they had been subjected to a lengthy "Attitude is every-thing" lecture; they had a better sense of how Tim was not living up to the coach's expectations. Several of his team-mates would have been willing to share their perceptions with Tim if he had asked.

Sometimes it is vital to have the feedback of other people to gain perspective on a situation. Adrianna, for example, was puzzled at the difficulty she was having in obtaining a job. She applied to several firms and thought that she had interviewed well each time. She showed up on time for each interview with a crisp, well-written résumé and was able to answer questions intelligently and in a manner that highlighted her educational and job experience. Her education was relevant to her career goals, and she was able to point this out to her employers. Proud of her striking appearance, she dressed stylishly for each inter-view in a way that emphasized her figure. She wore bright colors and plenty of makeup and did her hair in a daring, chic style.

The first few times that she was rejected she chalked it up to experience, knowing that it often takes many inter-views to land a good job. Correctly, she told herself that although she was well qualified, there might be many reasons why others would be chosen ahead of her. She realized that other might have even more experience, education, specialized training, work schedule flexibility, and so on.

After numerous interviews without favorable results, however, Adrianna started wondering if there might not be something that she could be doing better. Her brain-storming to explain why she wasn't being hired looked like this:

- Scuff marks on shoes.
- Aiming too high for a starting job.
- Firms I've applied to prefer to promote from within.

- Not enough connections in the business world.
- Rampant sex discrimination.
- Not enough business classes on my transcript.
- Letters of recommendation were not what I expected.

Adrianna's brainstorming list gave her some ideas for improving her chances of employment. She decided that it wouldn't hurt to take a few extra classes if that's what it took, or to start in a lower-level job and work her way up. She thought of double-checking with the people who were writing her letters of recommendation to make sure that what they said about her was favorable. She even considered consulting the Equal Employment Opportunities Commission* about the possibility that companies were refusing to hire her because of her gender. She figured that polishing her shoes for future interviews wouldn't hurt, either.

Adrianna's breakthrough came, however, when she decided to ask the people with whom she had interviewed why they had chosen not to hire her. That was a gutsy step for Adrianna, and it took a while for her to handle her stress about it. When she felt ready, she made the calls.

She had prepared what to say ahead of time: "Hi, this is Adrianna Robbins; I interviewed with you on June 13. I was wondering if you would tell me your impressions of my interview so that I can be better prepared for future interviews. I'm particularly interested in any comments you might have about things I could improve upon."

Several of the compaines that Adrianna called gave her

---

*The Equal Employment Opportunities Commission enforces laws that prohibit employment discrimination on the basis of race, color, religion, sex, or national origin.

vague or general feedback: "You were just fine, but we found someone a little better qualified." Two or three, however, gave her very specific feedback: Her qualifications were fine, but the company was very conservative and Adrianna's image didn't fill the bill. One woman even gave her examples concerning her clothing, hair, and makeup. This information, although hard to swallow, was particularly helpful to Adrianna because she would never have thought of it on her own. With this information to work with, she had a new option: She could tone down her image to improve her chances of being employed. For Adrianna, it was worth making the changes, and it helped her to land a job. Asking for outside information was crucial to her success.

Brainstorming is an excellent way to focus on the source of a problem and to creatively examine why it has occurred. If you brainstorm alone, however, the method has a limitation: Only one "brain" is involved in the "storming." There are always many ways to see a problem, and you may not want to limit yourself to the ideas that you can come up with on your own.

Consider Hank, who was raised by a mother who drank heavily. She was very critical of Hank, and he never quite felt that she liked or approved of him. As he tried to gain her acceptance, he worked hard in many areas. His brainstorming to explain why he felt rejected by his mother looked something like this:

- I don't get good enough grades.
- I don't do enough chores around the house.
- I don't look like my mother.
- I'm not good enough in sports.
- I'm not cheerful enough.

Hank was raised to believe that when his mother was drunk and angry it was all his fault. He had never been exposed to other possibilities. Because he had never talked to other people about the rejection he felt at home, he never got new perspectives on the situation.

A turnaround for Hank came when he joined AlAnon, a support group for family members of alcoholics. When he asked his friends in this group how they might explain his feelings of rejection, he was able to consider some different perspectives. The ideas they expressed were similar to these:

- Your mother says things she doesn't mean when she's been drinking.
- Your mother wants you to be perfect to make up for the problems in her life that she has caused by her drinking.
- Your mother doesn't know how to tell you what she likes about you because she never learned how to express her good feelings.
- You feel rejected because you try too hard to please someone who will never be satisfied.
- Your mother likes to focus on you to take the focus off of her own shortcomings.

These ideas would never have occurred to Hank. Having these perspectives influenced the ways in which Hank could cope with rejection. Now he could act not only on his own hunches but on other ideas that made sense to him.

Asking for outside opinions and brainstorming are ways to increase your understanding. In situations involving rejection these solutions may offer new insights and point to new directions for change. Understanding a situation can help in deciding how to cope with it.

Once you have an idea about how or why a rejection has occurred, the next step is to decide what to do about it. A mistake that people often make is to do nothing. Change can be intimidating, and people often forget that if what they are trying is not working, they can *do something different*. If you keep on trying new ways of coping, chances are good that you'll hit on something that works. Simple but true, these facts are easily forgotten.

When possible sources of a problem are generated by brainstorming, each idea that is created can be used as a starting point for brainstorming possible solutions. Hank, for example, might use some of the ideas brainstormed by his support group to find ways of coping with the rejection that he feels. His brainstorm solutions might go something like this:

> *Mom doesn't know how to tell me what she likes about me.*
> - Don't believe that just because Mom can't see my good qualities they are not there.
> - Stop blaming myself for Mom's bad moods.
> - Ask Mom directly what she likes about me.
> - Make friends who are able to say what they like about me.
>
> *Mom wants me to be perfect.*
> - Tell myself that I'm okay even if I'm not perfect, as long as I've tried my best at the things that are important to me.
> - Point out to Mom that I try my best.
> - Talk to school counselor about frustration with Mom.

- Ask Mom if I can take piano lessons on Fridays when she usually complains about me the most.
- Talk to my support group for more ideas.

Hank was able to expand on the ideas of his group to find solutions. Adrianna might have done that also with the feedback she received from the companies that did not hire her. Her brainstorms might have looked something like this:

Need more conservative image.
- Consult with several professional women to discuss what to wear to next interview.
- Talk with hairdresser to discuss appropriate styles.
- Go to library for books on interviewing.
- Look into support group for professional women to have someone to consult about things like this as they come up in the future.
- Talk to my friends who are in the field that I want to be in and see if they will come shopping with me to pick out a new interview suit.

Note that both Hank and Adrianna brainstormed ideas for getting outside help. Just as it can be useful to ask other people why a rejection might have occurred, it can also be useful to get outside help in generating solutions.

Understanding why a problem has occurred and developing ways to solve it are necessary steps in making changes. Brainstorming and consulting with others are excellent ways to begin.

CHAPTER ◇ 6

Taking Small Steps

C oping with any kind of problem can involve making changes. In coping with rejection, it would often be a relief if the changes could occur in other people or things. When it seems that something outside of yourself is causing you to feel unaccepted, it would feel wonderful to be able to make it change. Generally, however, that is not possible. Finding better ways to cope with problems more often entails searching for things that you can change about yourself. Those might include finding better ways of managing your emotions, or more closely examining your role in the experience. You might want to change how you look at problems, the effort you put into finding new friends, or the things you tell yourself in a difficult situation. Sometimes change involves taking a hard look at personal areas that you would like to improve.

In making changes, it is useful to have a goal. A goal starts with a problem that needs solving. Since the same situation can result from different kinds of problems for different people, an important first step in making changes is to identify the problem. For example, if both Beth and Alicia are feeling rejected because they were not invited to a party, each may have different reasons for the feeling; each may have a different problem that needs solving. If Beth was not invited because she lost her temper and told off the person giving the party, she may see her temper as the problem. If Alicia wasn't invited because she is shy, she may see her difficulty in speaking up as a problem.

Although everyone has personal areas that could use improving, spotting them can be hard. People can trick themselves out of facing problems in many ways.

One way is to minimize or ignore the problem. Pretending that a problem doesn't exist makes it easier to put off making a change. Beth, for example, might tell herself that her temper isn't a problem—people just make her angry a lot! Alicia might tell herself that she's fine, that her quiet personality is charming.

Another trick people use to avoid facing problems is to tell themselves that they are really okay. Alicia's shyness may be eating her up inside, but as long as she tells herself that she can live with being "just a little bit quiet," she doesn't have to face her feelings or work to change them. Beth may tell herself that she's proud of her ability to put people in their place, even if she is feeling out of control.

Blaming a shortcoming entirely on someone else is another way to avoid facing it. Alicia could tell herself that she is rarely invited out because her classmates are all stuck-up or conceited. Beth could tell herself that she often loses her temper because her classmates are aggravating, obnoxious pests.

People refuse to face problems that are contributing to rejection for many reasons. Some think that avoiding a problem will make it go away. Others have trouble facing parts of themselves that they don't feel good about. Pretending that problems don't exist or don't matter or blaming them on someone else are not useful ways of changing them.

To define a personal problem, you must be comfortable in admitting that it exists. You can begin by deciding to feel good about yourself even after you find personal areas that need improvement. All people have problems that make it hard for them to feel accepted under certain circumstances, or that make them overreact to an experience. Everyone has things about themselves that they would like to improve. Those people who can admit having room for improvement, and still feel good about themselves are the most likely to be able to identify their problem areas and change them.

Once you have given yourself permission to have areas that could use improvement, you can go about identifying them. Think about times in your life when you felt rejected. What did they have in common? What was happening? What were you saying to yourself? What were you feeling? What got in the way of feeling good about yourself? What did you do? Who else was involved? Look for things that were the same about each situation. That will give you clues to what might have been done better.

Three general problems often occur for people coping with rejection. One is overreacting emotionally to the feeling of rejection; instead of taking care of natural feelings, you make yourself feel worse by treating yourself badly. The second is ignoring patterns in experiences of rejection and the ways in which you might have contributed to them. The third is excessive fear of rejection that makes the situation worse. Thinking back over past experiences with rejection may help you to identify one or more of these problems.

If Leanna thinks about the last few times that she felt rejected, for example, she will recall that each case involved a night during the week on which her boyfriend did not call her. She will remember crying and telling herself that he was probably seeing someone else. She will remember that in each case her boyfriend had a good reason for not calling and that she felt very silly afterward. As Leanna mulls over ways to better cope with rejection, it might occur to her that she needs to monitor what she says to herself when her boyfriend doesn't call so as not to overreact. She may identify her insecurity with her boyfriend or her tendency to overreact as problem areas that need addressing.

If Angela thinks about the last few times that she felt rejected, she might recall four separate instances. In one case her best friend, Karen, went shopping with another friend and didn't invite Angela to go. In another case Karen didn't invite her to go bowling. In two other cases, Karen was busy with other plans when Angela called to see if they could get together. Angela felt left out on these occasions and wound up spending the whole day alone.

Angela may find that all of the times she felt rejected centered around the same person. She may come to question whether or not she is increasing her chances of feeling rejected by depending too much on her best friend for entertainment. Alternately, she may decide that she is contributing to the problem and that she needs to work on speaking up more where her friend is concerned. By identifying this pattern of feeling rejected, Angela can move on and generate possible solutions.

If Derrick thinks about the last three times he felt rejected, he will remember that in each case he asked someone for a date and was refused. Thinking about each situation, he will remember feeling self-conscious and embarrassed even before he approached the girl and telling himself that she would never go out with him. He might picture himself approaching the girls and realize that he never actually asked anyone anything. Instead he

dropped hints, beat around the bush, and finally left the situation, feeling that his worst fears of being rejected had come true.

Derrick may determine that he needs to work on being more self-confident and more straightforward. His fear of rejection was actually increasing the likelihood that it would happen. With this realization he can begin to set goals for himself.

Usually if you look closely at situations in which you have felt rejected, you will find that they have things in common— anything from who was present, to what you did or said to yourself, to what you chose to do about the situation, to how you chose to react emotionally. Identifying the commonalities can provide clues to what went wrong and what you might do differently in the future.

Finding a problem area to work on is the first step in finding a solution. Finding a solution involves setting a goal. A goal is something that answers the question, "What do I want to do differently?" A goal should be something that fits the problem. For example, if the problem is losing your temper, the goal may be learning to speak up before a situation gets out of control, or to take time out when you feel yourself getting angry.

From a goal, a plan can be generated. A plan answers the question, "Now that I have a goal, what do I need to do to make it happen?" For example, if Derrick had a goal to start feeling better about himself, he might plan to make a list of things that he likes about himself to read three times a day, or he might decide to sign up for a class in an area that interests him, to read a book on improving communication, or to hire a therapist. Because these plans are specific, Derrick will be able to tell when he has completed them. Because he will know when he has completed them, he will be better able to decide whether they have been helpful. Goals are more easily reached when plans are specific and realistic.

Similarly, it would not be enough for Angela to decide to make new friends or for Leanna to decide not to overreact to her boyfriend's not calling if they had no idea how to accomplish these goals. On the other hand, if Angela planned to say "Hi" to three new people a week, to ask one new person over to her house each week, or to join a new club, she would have a better sense of how to get started and would know when she had accomplished her goals.

If Leanna decided to get involved in after-school activities in order to feel more secure about herself, and to look into student government as well as choir and track, she would have a better sense of how to improve her situation and would be better able to recognize her accomplishments. She would have a plan.

Usually a plan works best when it is broken down into several small steps. It is easier to accomplish a simple small task than to struggle with a large difficult one. Further, when you can see that you are moving toward your goal, it is easier to stay on track.

Suppose that one of Derrick's goals to cope with feelings of rejection is to get a driver's license. He has decided that that will make him feel better about himself and increase his confidence in asking for dates. Derrick might divide his goal into steps as follows:

1. Find a driver's training school.
2. Get money to sign up.
3. Go to lessons.
4. Practice.
5. Take driving test.

Derrick now has several small manageable steps to work on. As he accomplishes each step, he will have reason to feel good about his progress. Derrick can make his plan even more manageable by dividing his five small steps into even smaller steps. His new list might look something like this.

1. *Find a driver's training school.*
   - Look in the Yellow Pages.
   - Ask teachers what schools they recommend.
   - Ask Bob what driving school he goes to.
   - Ask Cynthia what school she went to last year.
2. *Get money to sign up.*
   - Ask parents for a loan.
   - Count up money in savings.
   - Ask neighbors if I could cut grass or do chores for money.
   - Ask Shirley to pay back the money she owes me.
   - Ask parents to tell their friends that I'm available to baby-sit.
3. *Go to lessons.*
   - See if parents are willing to drive me.
   - Ask Mary if she wants to sign up for lessons at the same school and share rides.
   - Find a bus that goes by driving school.
4. *Practice.*
   - Ask older brother to practice with me.
   - Ask Dick (who has a license) to practice with me.
   - Ask Uncle Tim to practice with me.
   - Ask parents to practice with me.
5. *Take test.*
   - Set aside a half hour per night to study manual.

- Ask instructor what day test will be and mark it on calendar
- Find three ways to get to driving school on test date in case one of them falls through.

Any goal can be broken down into smaller steps that are easier to reach. Each time a step is taken, you come closer to reaching your goal and gain a sense of accomplishment. As each small goal in coping with rejection is reached, it is important to notice what has been accomplished and to feel good about it. Some people put their goals on paper so that as one is reached they can cross it off. They take great pleasure in watching their list grow shorter as items are crossed off. They also find that a list serves as a reminder of what they want to accomplish and a monitor of their progress.

Some people give themselves a little present or do something nice for themselves as they cross off or accomplish their goals. In this way they keep themselves feeling good about their accomplishments. However you keep track of your goals, it is important to focus on your successes.

Too many people make themselves miserable by focusing only on shortcomings rather than what they have accomplished. Focusing on failure leads to discouragement, and discouragement makes it harder to reach a goal. After an experience with rejection, focusing on failure can be particularly discouraging. Focusing on successes makes goal-setting fun.

Sometimes goals are not reached, but that does not necessarily mean that a failure has occurred. Nonetheless, it is useful to examine your progress toward your goals from time to time. When goals for coping with rejection are reached, take note of what you did right for future reference. When goals are not being reached, it is always useful to ask yourself why.

Sometimes goals are not being reached because they have been set too high. Rather than trying to lose five pounds or make a new friend, you set a goal to look like a model or to be the most popular person at school or work. When such goals are not reached, they merely need to be scaled down and made more practical.

Sometimes a goal is within reach, but the plan to get there needs to be reworked. Alicia may set a goal of meeting the two new students in her art class, but her plan to ask them to an outdoor activity is rained out. She might decide to change her plan to inviting them out for coffee or to a movie, or simply to spending a few extra minutes talking to them in class.

Sometimes both a goal and its plan are in good shape and within reason, but they are too easily forgotten. Emotional responses to rejection can make it hard to concentrate. Sometimes reminders are needed when a new goal is started. Reminders might be a note on a door or a refrigerator, a sign in a locker or car or on a notebook. Some people carry a picture of their goal—a photo of someone in peak physical shape to remind them to exercise, a picture of the friend that they want to remember to call. Some people use the old-fashioned string around the finger.

Sometimes a goal or plan is fine but has to wait because other goals or activities are more important. A goal of getting a job to raise money for a new hobby might have to wait until school is over. A goal of speaking to a friend about feeling rejected might have to wait until final exams are over. A goal of asking a friend on a date may have to wait until rehearsals for a choir performance are over.

No goal or plan needs to be set in stone; all can be

changed or revised, speeded up or slowed down, improved or thrown out as the situation requires. The important thing is to keep setting new goals and making new plans. Being honest in identifying problems and creating goals and plans to correct them helps in coping with any situation that involves rejection. Making a point of feeling good about progress and not dwelling on things that go wrong makes it easier to stick to a plan and to reach goals. Learning from successes as well as from mistakes makes goal-setting easier as you go along.

CHAPTER ◇ 7

Values

What would it be worth to you to learn better ways to cope with rejection? Would you be willing to take a new risk? Spend a little money? Give up some free time to learn a new skill? What else would you do? Would you give up a friend? Lie to your parents? Steal? Everybody has different standards. Sorting out what matters to *you* is an important consideration when deciding how to cope with an experience of rejection. These things that are important to you are called *values*.

Some people never stop to consider their values when deciding how to cope with rejection. They make plans for coping without stopping to think whether those plans will bring results that are in their best interests. Such people might give up a friend to better fit in with a new crowd without considering whether the friend is important to them. They might cling to a friend who regularly takes advantage of them without considering whether the relationship is bringing them the things they desire.

Because people value different things, similar situations might be handled successfully in very different ways by different people. If you are feeling rejected by a close friend with whom you have had an argument, you might cope with the situation by giving up a Sunday morning to get together with him or her and work it out. Somebody with strict religious beliefs might not feel comfortable giving up a Sunday morning, but might get together with the friend on a weekday. Yet another person might cope by picking up a book on communication skills and learning to communicate effectively so as to avoid arguments. Still another person might decide that the friend is not worthy of any effort and choose to cope with the situation by finding new acquaintances. None of these plans is right or wrong as long as it is the best solution for the person involved.

Priorities are the things that are most valuable to you, things for which you are willing to sacrifice less important things. When several things are important or valuable, choices have to be made. You may value both school and your friendships, for example, but place the importance of one above the other. Priorities determine which values come first.

Consider the trouble that could arise for people who don't know their priorities when it comes to deciding how to cope with rejection. Linda describes a problem that she had. "When I was sixteen, the really cool people in school wouldn't hang out with me. They were like in a world of their own. I noticed that most of them had cars, and I decided that if I had one I'd fit in better. I started working after school and on weekends, and as soon as I could afford a down payment, I got my car. It almost broke me though. I had to work every day and on weekends to make the monthly payments. I thought I was cool and all, but the people I wanted to notice me hardly ever saw me anymore. I never had time to *do* anything. I was tired all the time, and my grades started to suffer.

"Looking back, I'm not sure it was worth the time, money, and energy to get that car. If I were doing it again, I think I'd forget the car and just work on feeling better about myself and being confident. Maybe I'd spend some money on nicer clothes, or maybe just forget the popular crowd altogether and hang out with people who cared about me."

Linda ran into difficulties when she acted without considering her priorities. If she had stopped to think, she might have concluded that having energy, good grades, and time to have fun in high school were more important than buying a car. She might have decided that finding ways to like herself was more important than finding ways to make others like her.

Different things are important to different people. What is important to *you* is something that only you can decide. Knowing which of your overall values are most important can give you general guidelines for confronting and coping with situations involving rejection. The following are examples of the types of priorities that people have set for themselves.

TONY

1. Being true to my religion.
2. Getting good grades.
3. Getting along with my family.
4. Having good friends.

JEANNE

1. Being a professional dancer.
2. Being independent and standing up for myself.

3. Keeping my boyfriend.
4. Making new girlfriends.

ROBERT

1. Getting into shape.
2. Being popular at school.
3. Making the swim team next fall.
4. Getting my own apartment after graduation.

Having a personal list of priorities can be useful in making difficult decisions, including those that have to do with coping with rejection. Picture this scenario. You have paid for a modern dance class that meets every Thursday. Your current steady, a top swimmer on the school team, wants you to skip a dance class to come to the meet. Your team is favored to win. S/he threatens to break up if you don't go, and you know that you will feel rejected if that happens. On the same Thursday one of your friends is having a get-together and wants you to come early to help set up for it. To complicate things even further, your parents don't like for you to go out on week nights because it might interfere with your grades.

How do you decide what to do? Which of your values do you take into account in making your decision? Sorting out values can take some time. In this scenario the values that you might have to prioritize, or put in order, might include the following, to name a few:

1. The importance of pleasing your steady.
2. The importance of dancing.
3. The importance of following through on an interest that you have spent money on.
4. The importance of being at the party.

5. The importance of making independent decisions.
6. The importance of pleasing your parents.
7. The importance of pleasing your friend.
8. The importance of the swim meet.
9. The importance of your grades.

In what order would you place these values? How would your order be different from those of Tony, Jeanne, or Robert? What other values would you add as important considerations in this example?

What values would you take into account in making a decision about the following situation? Imagine that you are turned down for a job, and an employer tells you that you need more specialized course work to prepare for the position you are seeking. She suggests a summer class that costs $40. You had been hoping to spend most of your summer at a fine arts camp, honing your skills and making new friends. Which of your values would go into making this decision? Possible priorities could include the relative importance that you place on finding a job, the state of your finances, your dedication to fine arts, and the value that you place on meeting new friends.

Your future goals might enter into your decisions when setting priorities as well. Long-term goals can help you in deciding how to use your resources, which can help when it comes to coping with day-to-day situations of rejection. If college is a primary goal for you, for example, you might direct your efforts to feeling good about yourself by achieving good grades, as opposed to a plan that includes a lot of extracurricular activity. If your preference is to have friends in the future, you might opt to cope with a rejection by becoming more involved in people activities rather than spending time in solitude taking care of your emotions.

Some of your values will be priorities for life. Values can change, however. As people grow older and learn more about themselves and the world, certain things become more and less important. Emotional let-downs and crises such as those that can occur with rejection often push people to examine what is really important in their lives. Emotional challenges may help you to confirm that your values are truly important to you or may suggest that the time has come to look at the world a little differently and gain a new perspective on your priorities.

Precautions must be taken, however, if you push either of these ideas to its extreme. People who cope with rejection by forgetting their values may create new problems for themselves. They may act in ways that do not bring the results they desire. People with no sense of priorities sometimes act on impulse, without stopping to consider whether or not their choice of action will achieve what they want. Often this can lead to further rejection as others come to see them as irresponsible, immature, or too eager to please.

Marsha, for example, never thought about what it was worth to her to be in a high school clique. She only knew that it was important to her. She started spending all of her money on high fashion. When she didn't have enough money, she started shoplifting. She picked up the habits of the group and started snubbing people that they thought were "out." Marsha was not basically a snob or a criminal. However, she never considered whether she might have values that were more important. She never stopped to think whether being a friendly person who didn't steal might be more important than fitting in with the group. When the clique found out that she was stealing, they dropped her. When her old pals started to view her as a "fair-weather friend," they were no longer interested in her. Marsha lost out because she didn't think her values through.

At the other extreme, people with very rigid values may have a hard time recovering from an experience with rejection. When their old ways of solving a problem are not working, either because they have changed or they have come across a new situation, people with fixed values may get stuck. They may be unable to find new solutions because they are unwilling to question their values. They may encounter difficulties in being accepted by others with different values if they are not able to accommodate those values.

Marie, for example, had very fixed ideas concerning what she wanted in a date. He was to be tall, athletic, attractive, traditional, not too serious, and willing to spend money on her. Additionally, he was to be in the same career field as she was and of the same race and religion. Marie had other specific criteria as well, including political interests, age, hobbies, and recreational pursuits. She saw no compromise for these values. If people didn't meet her criteria, she dropped them. Needless to say, she rarely dated. Because her values were inflexible, she missed out on a lot of worthwhile relationships.

Paul had very specific values concerning what kind of job he would accept for summer employment. He wouldn't work in restaurants, in retail stores, in jobs that involved manual labor, or in any other kind of job that he felt was "beneath" him. The importance of this value didn't change even when he was turned down for several positions. He very much wanted to work and earn money, but this value did not allow him to do so.

As you make decisions involving sorting out your values in a rejection situation, it is important to be aware of the choices that you have. Often more choices are available than you first realize. Taking time to brainstorm alternatives can sometimes open your eyes to solutions to a problem that you hadn't thought of. Sometimes possible solutions are ignored because the person doesn't take time to think through the trade-offs involved. People may believe that the trade-off for coping with rejection in a new way would be too high, or that their values wouldn't allow it, but never stop to really think about it.

Damon believes that he could "never" cope with rejection by his peers by joining a club outside of school. If he stopped to think about it, he would realize that the reason for his feeling is his anxiety about meetings. If he joined a group, he would have to trade in the sense of security that he receives from never having to face an unknown group. He would be devoting time and energy to an activity with an uncertain outcome. If he doesn't take part in outside activities, he doesn't have to give up time and energy for something that might be unpleasant, and he might feel safer. He could take no risks and remain comfortably unhappy among his rejecting, yet predictable peers.

A closer look at Damon's situation, however, should reveal that he still has the choice of joining clubs. Though he believes that he "couldn't," it is more accurate to say that he considers the trade-offs too high. With a little more thought, Damon might reevaluate whether it is worth it to trade away the possibility of meeting new friends for the safety of remaining less anxious among rejecting peers.

Sometimes taking a look at your choices can allow you to have a better understanding of what is important to you. Brainstorming options for coping with rejection can provide a greater understanding of your values. Careful attention to values can help you to be sure that your values are neither too rigid nor too vague.

Values that belong to someone else can create pitfalls when you apply them to your own circumstances. Jacob's father is a Republican, and he automatically votes the same way. Maria's mother harbors prejudice against various ethnic groups, and so Maria does, too. Silvia's girlfriends all want to get married right after high school and become housewives, so Silvia tries to do the same thing.

Coping with rejection using someone else's set of values creates its own problems. You may occasionally find that someone else's values work well for you. More often, however, you will be displeased with the results. Imagine, for example, that Maria is trying to cope with rejection and turns up her nose at people of different ethnicities who try to help her; or that Jacob meets new friends after a brush with rejection, but they're all going to a Democratic convention; or that Silvia meets a man who is perfect for her but doesn't want to get married. Acting according to someone else's values can keep you from obtaining for yourself the things that are truly valuable to you.

From time to time it can be useful to ask yourself, "Am I making decisions that are consistent with my own priorities and values?" If the answer is no, it may be time for a change in action or a time to take another look at your priorities and values. Jessy, for example, placed the importance of time with his friends over time spent with his family. When he realized that he was spending most of his time at home, feeling bored and left out, it was time for a change in action. Don, who had similar priorities and was also spending a great deal of time at home, came to recognize that he was enjoying it, that he valued time with his family above that with his friends. It was time for him to rethink his values.

Sometimes actions become confusing when two values compete with each other. Lydia was always shy at parties, even though she highly valued speaking up and meeting people. She often came home feeling disappointed and rejected because she had kept to herself. Clearly her values and decisions were not consistent. When she gave the matter some thought, she realized that she was devoting a good deal of time and energy toward not looking foolish! The value of not looking foolish was competing with her value of speaking up—and it was winning! She reorganized her priorities; and though she occasionally makes a social blunder, she feels less rejected after parties because she speaks up and makes new friends.

It is important to consider your values and priorities to determine what solution is right for you. Sometimes just knowing that you have stuck with your values and priorities can make a situation easier. Perhaps you don't feel so bad about being rejected by a group that wanted you to shoplift, or a friend who you felt took you for granted. Maybe you feel good about being left out by people who expect you to be racially prejudiced or want you to do things that your values don't allow. Sometimes people feel that they have been rejected when in fact they have made a decision that was best for themselves but have not given themselves credit.

Brian was a college student. None of his high school friends had chosen to go on to higher education, and most were working at low-level jobs. Because most of them were living at home and had few expenses, they often got together for weekend trips that Brian couldn't afford. After asking him to go several times, his crowd eventually stopped inviting him.

At first Brian's reaction was to feel left out and rejected. When he started to think about the situation, however, he realized that he had choices. He could drop out of school if he wanted to, or he could let his grades slide and take a part-time job for extra money. When he realized that neither of those choices fit with his highest priority of finishing college, he felt better. He felt less rejected and more that he had made a positive choice.

With attention to your priorities and values problems can be handled successfully in different ways. For example, Bob and Allan were friends who were both taking flak from their schoolmates for being overweight. Bob decided that he valued speaking up for himself more than changing his behavior to suit others. He handled his situation by letting his classmates know exactly what he felt about their rude behavior and by choosing his friends more carefully. Allan decided that he valued fitting in more than the benefits that he gained from overeating, and he opted to cut back on calories and start exercising. Both were pleased with the outcomes because they acted in accordance with what was really important to them.

At times decisions about values are hard to make. It may be time to reevaluate your values or the way you have been sticking to them. It may be that you need to take a closer look at the trade-offs in how you are spending your time, energy, money, and other resources to make sure that you're not working against your best interests.

When you are making decisions that are consistent with your own best interests, you are better able to decide how to cope with rejection. You may begin to discover that rejection by people who are not concerned with your best interests is not such a bad thing.

CHAPTER 8

Feeling Good

A high level of self-confidence can go a long way in coping with and preventing some forms of rejection. A confident attitude helps to put others at ease. When you present yourself as a person who feels good about himself or herself, people are more likely to treat you as someone to feel good about. If you treat yourself like someone who is an embarrassment, people are likely to follow your lead and treat you accordingly.

Imagine that you invite a new friend to a party. The friend says, "I'd love to go! It sounds like a lot of fun. I can't wait to meet your friends!" You ask a second friend to come along, and that friend says, "I don't know. I won't know anyone. They might not like me and I might not fit in." Which friend would you most want to spend the evening with?

Perhaps you choose the person who seemed more confident. Something in the reply of the first friend might have told you that his or her outlook was, "I like myself, and I'm sure that you and your friends will like me too." The attitude of the second friend was more along the lines of, "I'm not very confident, so don't expect much of me. I might

73

make people feel uncomfortable. Don't expect me to add much to your party."

Feeling bad about yourself can start a negative cycle of events. You begin to feel down on yourself. Without knowing it, you may transmit this negative attitude to others. They begin to think of you as you think of yourself and to distance themselves from you. You begin to feel rejected and to lose your confidence. As you lose confidence you feel worse about yourself, and the negative cycle continues.

Imagine how this might occur on a job search. DeeAnn's first few job interviews go something like this:

Interviewer: So, DeeAnn, how were your grades last semester?

DeeAnn: Oh. Um. Not very good. I got a D in history. I really bombed.

Interviewer: Uh-huh. What kind of work-related experience have you had?

DeeAnn: Well, uh, I've never really had a job.

Interviewer: I see. How do you think you might get along with my office staff?

DeeAnn: Um. I don't know. Probably okay, I guess. I'm pretty shy, though.

What do you think about DeeAnn's chances of nailing a job? Poor, perhaps? DeeAnn sounds as if she does not feel very good about herself or very sure that she can do the job. Chances are good that the interviewer will pick up on that and treat her as a person who indeed cannot do the job. After several interviews that do not result in a job offer, DeeAnn may become discouraged and lose even more self-confidence. Potential bosses may pick up on this even more easily and become even less likely to offer her a job, and the negative cycle continues.

How could DeeAnn turn this around? One of her difficulties seems to be that she focuses on her negative qualities rather than on her favorable qualities. With the same qualifications and a dose of self-confidence, picture how DeeAnn could turn around her job interview by focusing on her strong points;

Interviewer: So, DeeAnn, how were your grades last semester?

DeeAnn: Overall, I was very pleased. I got an A in math and a B+ in Spanish. I ran into a little trouble in history, but I've spoken to my teacher and worked out a plan to raise my grade. I like school and enjoy getting good grades.

Interviewer: What kind of work-related experience have you had?

DeeAnn: I've had several opportunities to gain work-related experience. I've been a baby-sitter. I volunteered to do office work at school and learned to use a word processor. I was also on a swim team, which taught me the importance of being on time, of trying your best, and of working as a team. I'll be bringing the knowledge and skills that I gained at these experiences to my first job.

Interviewer: How do you think you might get along with my office staff?

DeeAnn: I can't see that there would be any

problems. I follow directions and I work
quickly. I tend to get along with people,
especially once I've had a chance to get
to know them.

In the second interview DeeAnn concentrates on her
good qualities. She is honest about her weak areas but
doesn't dwell on them. In all likelihood a potential boss
would be far more likely to hire DeeAnn when she pre-
sents herself with this confident attitude.

To develop a positive attitude about yourself, it is important to be aware of your good points. That does not
mean that you need to brag or boast. Having a positive
attitude about yourself means liking yourself for your
strengths and accepting your faults. Your confidence lets
people know that they need not be constantly concerned
about how to approach you so that you do not feel put down
or rejected. It allows people to relax and enjoy you.

Being aware of your positive traits can help you in
another way. Knowing your strengths and interests can
help you to find a common ground with other people.
Consider how Robert, who stays focused on his negative
traits, might react with a girl he has just met:

Lana: Pleased to meet you, Robert. What do you
         like to do for fun?
Robert: Oh, I uh, not much.
Lana: Oh. Well, would you like to dance?
Robert: Um, no. I'm not a very good dancer.
Lana: Me either. That's okay. We can dance over
         there in the corner.
Robert: I'd feel silly.
Lana: Oh. Okay. Hey, Tony . . . !

With the focus on his abilities and interests, Robert might have found some common interests to share with Lana and might have made a new friend:

Lana: Pleased to meet you, Robert. What do you like to do for fun?

Robert: Well, I like music. I'm learning to play the sax, and I just picked up a new jazz CD.

Lana: Really? I've been singing since I was little, mostly in choir, but I've always liked jazz and blues, too.

Robert: You know, I'm not the greatest dancer, but I'd sure like to dance with you.

Lana: Ah, something else we have in common! I'm not the greatest dancer either, but I suppose we can take turns leading. Let's go!

To be able to focus on your good points, you must be aware of what they are. Your positive qualities might include your current skills, your interests or ideas, your past successes, your future goals. To identify your strengths, you may want to look at all the different areas of your life: school, work, sports, personality, values, appearance, hobbies, beliefs, etc.

Take time to list all the things that you like about yourself. Most people have more strong points than they are aware of. Some examples might look like this:

Paul's List
  Sports
    I'm good at hockey.
    I exercise at home once a week.
    I like watching football on TV.
    I like watching gymnastics on TV.

I won a medal for a race in high school.
I am learning to swim.
I taught some younger kids to play dodge-ball.

School

I like math.
I'm taking French next year.
I got an A on my geometry final.
Most of my teachers like me.
I'm pretty good in English.

Appearance

I have good taste in clothes.
People tell me that I have nice eyes.
I like my haircut.
I stay in decent physical shape.

Morals

I'm good to animals and to my pets.
I feel good about my religious beliefs.
I can keep a secret.
I don't get into many arguments.
I feel good about the volunteer work that I did
    two years ago.
I can stand up for myself when I have to.

Maria's List

Work

I am always on time.
I got a raise last year.
My boss told me that she thinks I'll be a manager
    one day.
I always do extra projects if I finish up early.
I work quickly.
I do well with computers.

I'm nice to the people I work with.
I rarely take sick days.

Hobbies
I am proud of signing up for a martial arts class.
I took a computer class last year.
I am glad that I have interests outside of work. I
think they make me more interesting.
I like to read.
I like to keep a diary and to write poetry.

Personality
I don't let people take advantage of me.
I'm working on not being so shy.
I am respectful of other people.
I have future goals for myself.
I like the fact that I can accept my shortcomings.
I like to party.
I'm the kind of person who always likes to try
something new.

Use your imagination when you develop your own list.
Let the categories and items go on and on. No strength is
too small to be aware of.

Some people get stuck after the first few items. They
may not be used to focusing on their good points, or
perhaps they focus too much on their bad points. If that
happens to you, stop for a moment. Choose one of the good
points you have listed and ask yourself, "What are the
positive qualities of a person who has this strength?" For
example, if you listed, "I am good at hockey" and you considered the skills and traits that a good hockey player might
possess, you might realize that you have other favorable
qualities. You might then list, "I am good at skating," "I'm

in good physical condition," "I'm good at strategy," "I'm a good sport when I lose," "I work well on a team." Each of these new items might then remind you of even more of your strong points.

Consider how Linda might expand on her list:

Linda's original list
  Interests
    I'm good at singing.
    I like to style my hair.
    I like to spend time with my friends.

Linda can use these original ideas to become aware of other strong points. When she asks herself, "What are the good qualities of a person who has these strengths?" her expanded list might look like this:

I'm good at singing.
    I have a clear voice.
    I can read music.
    I practice hard at things that I am interested in.
    I'm not afraid to try new things.
    I know a lot about music and songwriters.
    I have an awesome record collection.
    I'm not afraid to perform in front of an audience.

I like to style my hair.
    I have a keen sense of style.
    I have clean shining hair.
    My hair is a pretty shade.
    I know how to make myself look well.
    I have good taste.

I like to spend time with my friends.
    My friends like and respect me.

I choose my friends carefully.
On weekends I keep pretty active.
I know how to keep a secret.
I'm the kind of person that friends can trust.

From here Linda can expand her list further, using her new items to generate even more ideas. She might use the item, "I am the kind of person that people can trust," to remind herself that she also possesses the following traits: "I don't lie to my friends," "I don't talk behind people's backs," "I share with my friends when I can," "I tell my friends when something they do bothers me."

Skills or interests that can be developed further should always be included on your lists. Making a point of further developing these skills and interests can be another way of feeling good about yourself and of finding common interests with other people.

Take a class in an area that interests you: poetry, business, learning to communicate or organize more effectively, auto mechanics, embroidery, modeling, baseball, art history, jogging, model building, swimming, cooking, first aid, Spanish.

Books are also excellent sources of information for developing new skills and interests. Reading can help you to develop an interest in everything from rock music, to classic cars, to European culture, to politics, to baseball.

Another way to develop interests and increase your self-confidence is to do volunteer work. Hospitals, charity organizations, day-care centers, businesses, crisis hotlines, and libraries often need responsible volunteers. Volunteer work provides the opportunity to learn new skills and to increase your sense of importance. Chosen carefully, volunteer work can also help you to learn about or prepare for a career choice or advancement.

Taking steps to develop and expand upon interests and improve self-confidence involves a certain amount of risk and practice. Change usually takes time and is a little bit scary; no one becomes perfect overnight. It takes courage to risk trying new things.

Taking risks might mean sharing your interests with someone new, joining a new club, or taking a class in an area that you're not familiar with. With each risk taken comes the possibility of failure. Like anything else, taking risks and accepting failures can be easier when you focus on what you did well, not on what went badly. Remind yourself of at least one positive trait whenever a risk you take does not work out the way you had planned.

What could be a positive thing to find in yourself after you take a risk that causes you to fall flat on your face? How about, "I am willing to try new things," or "I am a risk taker," or "I'm the kind of person who can learn from this experience," or "I am very brave to have risked trying this," or "I am glad to have this practice experience out of the way." Many positive traits are to be found in people who take risks even when things don't turn out as planned. In the long run, people who have taken the most risks will have the most successes.

In any situation in which you feel rejected, usually someone or something else is involved. Don't overlook your own contribution to the experience or your own responsibility for your feelings. However, remember also to take a look at the other factors involved.

Imagine that a potential date says no. You may want to look at your attitude, your communication, your hygiene— whatever! Then consider the outside factors that were involved. Was s/he preoccupied? Snooty? Indifferent to the feelings of others? Not interested in the place that you wanted to go for a date? Married? On drugs? If the situation involves someone else, *refuse* to feel bad for both of you. Always take the whole picture into account.

Eventually, of course, everyone finds a flaw in himself that cannot be changed. You may have a physical imperfection, or you may lack a particular skill even though you have truly tried to develop it. In this situation, it is important to do three things. First, give yourself permission to have a flaw; everybody does. Second, accept yourself flaws and all, and remember that the degree to which others accept or reject you will largely depend on the degree to which you accept or reject yourself. Third, once you have accepted flaws, don't dwell on them. Focus instead on your positive traits and develop them.

Eventually, all of us meet with rejection. It is important at such times to remember your good points, to accept your flaws, to consider all the factors involved, and to keep on trying.

Feeling good makes coping with rejection easier!

CHAPTER ◇ 9

Creating Confidence

Sometimes after an experience with rejection your confidence can take a nosedive. At such times it is useful to boost your confidence level. There are many ways to achieve that: successfully solving problems, learning to speak up for yourself, learning a new skill. Sometimes, however, confidence can be improved simply by practicing looking as if you feel confident.

People who are considered confident are often treated with more respect. Others may be more interested in meeting and getting to know them.

The way you present yourself physically makes a statement about how you feel about yourself. Your carriage, the expression on your face, and the distance that you put between yourself and other people are all ways of giving information about yourself to other people before a single word is spoken.

When Dion enters a room full of new people at a party, for example, she approaches an interesting person and looks him or her in the eye. Standing tall, she greets the person with a warm smile and an outstretched hand. She introduces herself in a calm, self-assured voice. Her approach spells confidence before her new friend knows anything about her.

Lisa, on the other hand, freezes up in the same situation. She folds her arms as if to protect herself and looks for a chair or a corner to disappear into. She often puts her purse on the chair next to her to keep strangers from sitting next to her. Slouched down in her chair, she hopes no one will look her way. If someone does, she stares at the floor or quickly appears interested in something else: a decoration perhaps, or the food tray.

Shyness is written all over Lisa's presentation. It is hard for potential acquaintances to approach her without scaring her off and making themselves feel foolish. Whereas Dion enjoys herself among people, Lisa comes away from group situations feeling rejected. What is it about Dion that allows her to convey to others that she is a confident young woman who is interested in having others get to know her? What is it about Lisa that gives the impression that she would rather be left to herself?

The easy answer is that Dion is a more confident person. Dion feels sure of herself, whereas Lisa is so focused on her flaws that she's sure everyone else is focused on them, too. That isn't the whole story, however. There are times when Dion is feeling down, and people still look forward to meeting her. There are times when Lisa feels great about herself, and no one seems to care. The crucial difference is in the styles that Dion and Lisa present.

Dion has mastered the art of *looking* confident no matter how she feels. In contrast, Lisa has nearly perfected the art of looking timid and shy. Dion's confident attitude gives others confidence in her and makes her appear more interesting. It assures them that a social encounter with her will be neither awkward nor embarrassing. Dion's way of presenting herself invites others to feel at ease with her, whether she is feeling confident or not.

Lisa's presentation, on the other hand, tends to make

others uneasy. People take her looking away from them as a sign that they are not interesting to her. Some guess her to be conceited or stuck-up. Some sense that she is shy but are afraid to approach her for fear they will be snubbed.

Both Dion and Lisa send signals that indicate how worthwhile they believe themselves to be. Dion's signals tell a room full of people that she believes herself to be a desirable person. Lisa's tell the world that she feels like a flop. Those receiving the signals use them to gage how worthwhile they will find these new people. But what are those signals?

Eye contact is an important signal. Looking someone in the eye makes a statement of interest. It tells another person not only that you are interested in him or her, but that you have the confidence to show your interest without fear of rejection.

Like any skill, making eye contact takes practice. Begin by being aware of where your eyes are focused when you are with another person. If you are unable to look others in the eye, look them in the face. Focus near the eyes in areas such as the forehead or bridge of the nose.

Once you have accomplished this skill, concentrate on increasing the time that you feel comfortable making eye contact. When you become uncomfortable and want to look away, hold your gaze for a few seconds longer. Notice what triggers you to look away. This is different for everyone. Some people feel intimidated when others return their gaze. Others feel that they are being disrespectful. Still others may look away when they run out of things to say.

Become mindful of what you are saying to yourself when you begin to be uncomfortable with eye contact. Are you thinking that the other person is becoming bored? That he or she is finding you unattractive? Uneducated? Dull? Be mindful of things that happen when you make eye contact. What does the other person do? Does he or she look back? How does that make you feel?

Sometimes when you make eye contact, the other person may feel shy or embarrassed and look away. Some socially awkward people may be annoyed. A more common reaction, however, is for the person to return the contact, often with a smile.

Together with eye contact, your facial expression can carry an attitude of confidence. A warm smile, for example, can make the statement that you are confident, pleasant, and willing to make contact. Smiling can be practiced. Some people are not aware of their facial expressions and need to practice in front of a mirror. What expression would you use to convey interest? Put it on and try it out. What expression would you use to convey affection? Curiosity?

Sometimes this exercise can lead to surprises. The smile that you thought was warm and friendly may actually look more like a leer. Perhaps your best look of confidence really looks snobbish, or your most "desirable" look has you puckered like a fish. Perhaps your expressions look artificial to you. Think of some warm thoughts. Imagine that you are about to meet a person who is interesting and friendly. Remind yourself of something that you particularly like about yourself. Facial expressions look more natural when they stem from real emotion or positive thoughts.

Another easy way to improve your appearance of confidence is to improve your posture. Standing in front of a mirror, try this exercise to demonstrate how big a difference that can make. First roll your shoulders forward and drop your chin. Put all your weight on one leg. You'll probably see your confident look disappear.

Next put your weight equally on both feet. Roll your

shoulders back and lift your chin about an inch higher than you usually carry it. Straighten your back. Presto! A more confident looking you, ready to take on the world!

When creating a confident look, guard against too much fidgeting. Nervous movements, such as playing with pencils or table utensils, pacing, playing with your hair all undermine a confident presentation. Some nervous movements, however, can be disguised. If your hands seem constantly to be playing with things, use them to gesture while you talk. A coin or a paper clip in a jacket pocket will allow you to fidget discreetly to your heart's content without ruining your confident look.

It is important not to put barriers between yourself and other people. A barrier can be created by putting a great deal of space between yourself and others; for example, sitting away from others at a party or sitting at a table while others are standing. Barriers can be actual objects such as a table or a snack tray, or they can be parts of your body. Some people create a barrier by folding their arms in front of them.

Barriers can be more subtle. Some people hide behind a drink, a cigarette, or a snack. They position themselves in such a way as to say, "Don't bother me, I am busy enjoying this drink (or whatever)." Others slump deep into their chair or hold things on their lap. Placing barriers between yourself and another person undermines a look of confidence. It says to others, "I'm not too sure of my abilities in this situation, so I'm putting this between us for my protection."

A person who is confident or learning to create confidence is learning to call the shots. When she wants an introduction, she introduces herself. When he feels it is time to go, he leaves. When she wants to dance, she asks someone to dance. When he wants to indicate that he is not interested, he turns away or puts up barriers. Taking the first steps and acting on decisions that you have made are ways of not only appearing confident, but becoming confident.

Sometimes, of course, you will encounter a negative reaction. Others may be shy, rude, socially awkward, or simply not comfortable with confident people. More often, however, people will respond favorably to your look of confidence.

The next time you are in a group, notice how others show confidence. Notice the posture, the facial expressions, and the eye contact of those who appear confident, and the effects on those around them. Becoming more aware of the signs of confidence will help you to develop them for yourself. As you become more comfortable with appearing confident, it will feel more natural. You will begin to feel as if you *are* confident rather than *acting* confident.

Confidence will have been created!

CHAPTER 10

Polishing "People Skills"

Very often, feelings of rejection stem from a relationship with another person. After an experience with rejection, some people feel a little gun-shy. It may be harder to feel confident in similar situations. After a breakup, for example, people may lose their confidence in approaching members of the opposite sex. People feeling rejected by a friend may have difficulty making new friends. Those with rejecting families may feel shy about facing people in general.

Learning to overcome the fear of being rejected again is an important step in coping with rejection. Paying close attention to your "people skills" can help you to build up the confidence needed to take new chances with people.

Many skills go into good relationships. Many of them can be learned the way you learn to ride a bike or drive a car. Among those skills are careful listening, starting and taking part in conversations, being considerate of others, and setting limits with other people. Like many other learned skills, they may feel awkward at first but become easier

POLISHING "PEOPLE SKILLS"

with practice.

One important skill is the ability to listen. Understanding people better is a way to avoid misunderstandings that can lead to rejection. Being a good listener can also be of use in making new friends. A good listener is usually greatly appreciated. People like to know that they are being heard and understood.

Being a good listener means not interrupting, not even to give advice or to share a similar story. It means encouraging a person to speak fully without judging or preaching. There are at least three levels of careful listening. At the first level you indicate to another person that you are aware that he or she is talking and want to hear what he or she has to say. At the second level you indicate that you *understand* what is being said. At the third level, you let the speaker know that you understand the *feelings* behind what is being said. On all levels, close listening involves keeping the conversation focused rather than changing the subject.

Small comments can let it be known that you interested in what is being said and are paying attention:

- Uh-huh.
- I see.
- Really?
- Go on.
- Neat!
- I see what you mean.
- You're kidding!
- Wow!

To show that you are understanding, you can repeat the main themes of what is being said to you, either exactly as you heard them or in your own words. Your end of the conversation might begin with phrases like the following:

- So what you're saying is . . .
- If I understand you correctly, you're telling me . . .
- What I'm hearing is that . . .
- So the way it happened was . . .
- You mean that . . .

At the deepest level of listening, you reveal an interest not only in the facts but in the feelings behind them. You let others know that you are attending not only to their words, but to their emotions. Your responses to a speaker might begin with phrases similar to the following:

- So you're feeling . . .
- You must feel . . .
- I wonder if you are feeling . . .
- That sounds . . .
- You seem . . .

A conversation at such a level might go something like this:

Lisa: I broke up with my boyfriend.
You: You sound disappointed.
Lisa: I am. We had some really good times together.
You: So you're upset.
Lisa: Well, I'm disappointed, but not really upset. We had differences, I guess.
You: So in a way, you are relieved?
Lisa: Yeah, in a way. I'm disappointed, but I am relieved too. It never would have worked out, considering the way he wanted things.
You: Mixed feelings, huh?
Lisa: Yeah. Overall I guess I'm optimistic, though. Hey, thanks for listening. I feel a lot better.
You: Sure thing.

It is not vital that you perfectly understand the person's feelings to show that you are earnestly concerned. As long as you are making a sincere effort to convey your understanding, others will often help you to understand their feelings. If you say that someone sounds sad, for example, the person may say it's not exactly feeling down, but exhausted from taking a test.

Of course, at times you will want not only to listen carefully but also to take a more active part in a conversation with new friends. A lot of people get stuck with this. Nearly everyone has had the experience, for example, of meeting a friendly or attractive person and becoming tongue-tied. Many have opened a conversation but not known what to say after the first few words. Sometimes people are so afraid of rejection that they say nothing. They may wind up having their fears realized if the new acquaintance misinterprets the lack of conversation as lack of interest.

Any conversation you have will depend on the other person's interest in you and, perhaps more important, on his or her conversational skills. These are factors over which you have no control. On your end, however, you can do several things to make a conversation happen.

An easy trick is to ask a question that requires more than a one-word answer. For instance, "Did you like the dance on Saturday?" will bring a response of either "Yes" or "No." In contrast, "What was your favorite part of the dance on Saturday?" will bring any number of longer, responses that may provide ideas for continuing the conversation.

Consider the difference that this simple idea would make in the following conversations. Imagine that you have decided to cope with an experience of rejection by making new friends. You go to a party and speak with a new acquaintance. Which conversation would you prefer to have?

SHORT-ANSWER QUESTION CONVERSATION

You: Are you from this area?

Niki: No. I am from Florida. Where are you from?

You: This is my hometown. Do you like Florida?

Niki: Yes. Do you like living here?

You: Yes.

LONG-ANSWER QUESTION CONVERSATION

You: What was the town like where you grew up?

Niki: It's really pretty. It is wooded, with a lot of places to swim. I really liked it.

You: Really? I like nature and the outdoors too. What kinds of things did you do for fun there?

Niki: Mostly camping, fishing, and hiking.

You: What was the most fun you ever had camping?

Niki: Well, there was the time that we all packed up and went down to...

Some people get stuck on what to ask about or what to say to start a conversation. Some simply introduce themselves and ask for the other person's name. Others offer a compliment, perhaps admiring a tie or a sweater. Some people simply begin by making a comment on whatever is obvious, "Looks like rain," for example, or "These checkout lines seem to take forever." Any of those openers can be followed up with a "long-answer" question.

Once a conversation has begun, it is not so important what you say. Most people respond well to friendly, respectful attempts to make contact. Attempts that are not successful can be written off as practice for a more suitable conversation partner. What you discuss will depend on your interests as well as those of the person with whom you

are talking. Since most people enjoy talking about themselves, "What do you think about...," or "What do you
like to do for fun?" or "How would you feel if..." are
usually good types of questions. The biggest mistake
people make in a conversation, however, is in failing to say
anything. Silence will kill a conversation quicker than
anything "wrong" you might say.

Killing a conversation can actually make you feel rejected. Picture this scenario: You've met someone new and
attractive at a party. You've said, "Hi." He or she says,
"Hi." The ball's in your court; it's up to you to say something—anything. You say nothing. The other person
doesn't know what to do. Perhaps s/he thinks that you're
not so interested after all; perhaps s/he thinks you were just
being polite. S/he gets embarrassed; you get embarrassed.
S/he leaves. You feel rejected. Sometimes simply practicing
the skills of speaking up in conversation can help you to
avoid feelings of rejection.

Many other skills go into being good with people. One is
treating people with respect, or the way they like to be
treated. That might involve granting an occasional favor, or
being polite, or helping someone to feel comfortable with
you. A rule of thumb is to treat people the way you would
like to be treated. Sometimes, however, it involves more
than that.

Treating people with respect often involves treating
them as *they* would like to be treated, even if that makes no
sense to you. People from other cultures or even other
neighborhoods or families may have very different ideas
about being respectful or considerate.

Bill's family is very laid back at dinner time. They are
often in front of the TV, feet up on the coffee table, sometimes using paper plates or eating directly from bags of fast
food. No one makes much of a fuss about table manners;

the whole affair is very casual. At Don's home, in contrast, dinner is a formal occasion every night. The table is properly set. Milk is served in a pitcher, not a carton, and the various dishes are placed in serving platters. Formal manners are the rule of the house.

Don thinks that Bill's family are slobs, and he might be right. Bill thinks that Don's family are particularly uptight, and he may have a point. Nonetheless, when they visit each other's homes they act in a way that makes the other feel comfortable. Don likes Bill to use his salad fork, and he does. Bill likes Don not to make a face when his mother offers him bread out of a bag instead of a basket, and he tries his best. Each of these friends is courteous to the other in ways that they would never expect and certainly would not want the other to return. The two get along just fine.

Different people like to be treated differently. One friend may be offended if you raise your voice with him, while another may be upset to know that you are angry and are not letting her know about it. One friend may want you to be on good terms with her boyfriend, while another may prefer to keep her other relationships private. Another friend may enjoy having you telephone almost daily, while someone else may feel pestered with as many as two calls a week.

Often it is possible to accommodate the wishes of others, even if they are different from your own. Compromise prevents feelings of rejection that can end a friendship. As long as your own rights or feelings are not compromised in the process, it can be rewarding to go out of your way for the sake of developing or maintaining a good relationship. If you feel that the line is crossed, however, it is up to you to set limits and to refuse unreasonable requests.

Along with respecting the preferences of others comes

respecting the preferences that *you* feel strongly about. The skill of setting limits with others is as important as the skill of helping them to feel comfortable. Some people feel that to avoid rejection, or to be liked, or to be polite they must grant any request. Such people often feel exploited or taken advantage of. They may find themselves doing things that they would rather not do and in some cases living with the negative consequences of those actions.

Think for a minute about your own limits. What are your limits sexually, for example? What would you do if someone wanted you to do things you were not comfortable with? How would you handle a person who wanted to borrow money from you? How much would be too much? How many unreturned favors are you willing to do for a friend before you start refusing to do more? What kinds of things are you willing to do to make a friend comfortable? What about an acquaintance? Are you willing to bend rules for a friend? Laws? How would you tell someone that you were not willing to do what was being asked of you?

Everyone has limits, and it is important to be aware of your own. When people are feeling rejected, however, or emotionally upset, they may be vulnerable to violating their own limits to please other people.

For example, when Marta's boyfriend broke up with her, she felt as if no one would ever be interested in her again. For a while after the breakup, the only person who asked her out was a guy she did not particularly care for, who kept pressuring her to do sexual things. Ordinarily, Marta would have dropped him like a hot potato, but at the time she was feeling an almost desperate need to be accepted in a romantic relationship. She told herself that he was the only person who would ever be interested in her and she went along with the sexual relations. Because Marta compromised her best interests and chose not to enforce her own limits, her style of coping with her boy-friend's rejection did not make her feel better about herself; it made her feel worse.

Saying no to someone or something is difficult for some people. When they are feeling rejected it can be doubly hard. Wanting to be accepted by someone, or by *anyone*, can make it harder for you to make decisions that you can live with. Thinking about your limits ahead of time and recognizing that you will sometimes need to enforce them can help you prepare to stand by the limits that are important to you.

When someone is trying to push you into doing something that you're not interested in, you can let that be known. Whereas careful listening and feedback encourage conversation, silence can effectively end a conversation; so can turning your back, or walking away. Or both. Although it may be preferable to speak up and state why you do not want to grant a request, these steps can act as back-up when you feel that someone is not respecting your limits.

In addition to the "people skills" discussed here, everyone has something of their own that others respond well to. It may be an interest, a strength, a way of understanding, a special facial expression, a sense of humor. It is up to you to find that special something and to let others know about it. Politeness, setting limits, developing good conversations, and many of the other things discussed in this book are skills that can be learned. The best parts of you, however, the parts that will be accepted and cherished by others, are up to you to discover and to develop.

CHAPTER 11

A Final Word:

When the Shoe is on

the Other Foot

R ejection is a part of life. Although many people have a hard time coping with difficult feelings when they have been rejected, some people have an equally hard time when *they* need to do the rejecting. You may face situations that require you to do the rejecting: you're in charge of casting for a school play; you decide to break up a relationship; you're in charge of hiring for a company.

Deciding that you do not want to be involved with someone may become easier if you remember that you are entitled to set limits for yourself. No one can be friends with everyone. People are simply too different to be all things to all people. Being sure of the limits that you have for the behavior of other people can help you to know when you need to part company.

Your values can also help you in this regard. They can let you know when you are needlessly rejecting someone versus keeping yourself from a detrimental relationship. This distinction is not always clear. If a friend gets in trouble, for example, at what point are you needlessly deserting a friend in need, and at what point are you maintaining a friendship that could hurt you? Decisions like that are hard to make and require that you closely examine the things that are important to you.

It is always important to look at the trade-offs in such a decision. When it is clear that the benefits of a relationship are not worth its negative aspects, the decision to bail out becomes easier.

Sometimes people are aware that they are maintaining a relationship that is harmful to them. They are aware that the negative trade-offs far outweigh the positive, yet they become stuck when it comes to ending or changing the relationship. There may be a small positive benefit of which they can't let go. For example, Dan was dating a girl who took him for granted and routinely saw other men. Dan's feelings for her had declined a good deal, and he no longer felt good about the relationship. However, he valued having a date every Friday night. Even though he knew that it was not reason enough to keep the relationship going, the thought of having nothing to do on Friday nights kept him from saying goodbye.

In situations like this, it can be useful to plan ahead for ending a relationship. Dan might have prepared for the breakup by planning other ways to spend Friday nights. He might also have planned ahead how to take care of any bad feelings he had about the breakup, such as paying close attention to what he was saying to himself about the situation, giving himself a little emotional first aid, or maybe talking to a friend.

Maing a decision to act in your own best interests requires confidence. It requires knowing that you are worthy of positive and fulfilling relationships. It is important to have confidence in your ability to think and act independently.

That is not to say, however, that you cannot talk things over with someone else before making a final decision about ending a relationship. Just as skills in expressing yourself can help in coping with your own feelings of rejection, they can help when it is you who needs to do the rejecting. Perhaps you have never before been in a position of having to reject someone, and you are experiencing new feelings that you need to discuss.

Expressing yourself is also important in coping with the person with whom you are parting company. Keep in mind that the person is probably feeling rejected. Useful things to tell the person are your reasons for ending the relationship and your feelings about his or her behavior.

Following through with a plan for ending or modifying a relationship can be easier if you know ahead of time what you are going to say. It can also be useful to think about what the other person might say or do and what you would do in response. Thinking through how the interaction might occur can make the situation less stressful. It can also be useful to have a plan for when and where you are going to act. If you have been putting off the rejection, setting a specific time and place can help you to confront the situation once and for all.

When ending or modifying a relationship or when you have to reject someone, it is useful to think about the feelings that he or she might be having. This can help you to be sensitive to the person's feelings and also to deal with any negative reactions. Picturing a "worst case" scenario can help you to feel prepared for anything.

If you are having trouble finding a way to reject someone, a good place to start is to imagine how you would like to have the situation handled if you were the person. In all likelihood, you would prefer to be treated with respect, for example.

Treating someone with respect means to avoid putting the person down in any way. If you limit your communication to what specifically makes you want to part company, your feelings, and what you expect from the relationship in the future, you will be more likely to avoid being disrespectful.

After you have rejected someone else, it may be necessary to take care of your own feelings. You may have an emotional reaction to the experience or to the person himself or herself. You may need to spend some time alone or to apply some emotional first aid. If you are feeling bad about the experience, it may be necessary to review how your decision was made and the reasons for it. By reviewing things that you did well—such as being respectful or expressing yourself clearly, and things that you would like to have done differently—perhaps choosing different words or discussing it sooner, you can learn from the experience.

It may be useful to remind yourself that having a relationship that turned out badly does not make you a bad person. It may be useful to look for things that you could have done differently to preserve the relationship, to avoid it in the first place, or to end it sooner.

No one likes having to reject another person. However, for most people there comes a time when someone in their life is not meeting their expectations. The person may be falling short in the role of friend, steady date, employee, or whatever. Because people are different, there will be times when two people cannot meet each other's expectations.

One of the two will have to be the one to part company.

Rejection is a normal part of life. When it happens to you, respect yourself enough to take care of yourself. When you must reject another person, care enough to be respectful of him or her.

Bibliography

Alberti, R.E., and Emmons, M.L. *Your Perfect Right*. San Luis Obispo, CA: Impact Press, 1974.

Baer, J. *How to Be an Assertive (Not Aggressive) Woman in Life, in Love, and on the Job*. New York: New American Library, 1976.

Beck, A.T., Rush, J.A., Shaw, B.F., and Emery, G. *Cognitive Therapy of Depression*. New York: The Guilford Press, 1979.

Bower, S.A., and Bower, G.H. *Asserting Yourself: A Practical Guide for Positive Change*. Addison-Wesley Publishing Company, 1989.

Ellis, A. "Love and Its Problems." In Albert Ellis and Michael Bernard, eds. *Clinical Applications of Rational Emotive Therapy*. New York: Plenum Press, 1985.

Krawetz, M. *Self-Esteem Passport*. New York: Henry Holtz and Co., Inc., 1984.

Lloyd, S.R. *Developing Positive Assertiveness*. Los Altos, CA: Crisp Publications, Inc., 1988.

Masters, J.C., Burish, T.G., Hollon, S.D., and Rimm, D.C. *Behavior Therapy*. Orlando: Harcourt Brace Jovanovich, 1987.

Osborn, A.F. *Applied Imagination*. New York: Scribners, 1957.

Ottens, A.J. *Coping with Romantic Breakup*. New York: The Rosen Publishing Group, 1985.

Rogers, C.R. *On Becoming a Person*. Boston: Houghton Mifflin, 1961.

Index